Head-Scratching, Eye-Catching (3-D) Conundrums

László Kresz
Károly Kresz
István Kresz

With a foreword by
László Mérő

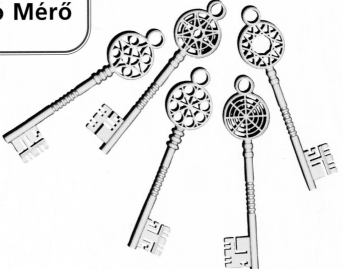

STERLING PUBLISHING CO., INC.
New York

Library of Congress Cataloging-in-Publication Data

Kresz, László.
    [Látványos fejtörok. English]
    Head-scratching, eye-catching, 3-D conundrums / László Kresz, Károly Kresz,
    Is[t]ván Kresz.
        p. cm.
    Includes index.
    ISBN 1-4027-1823-3
    1. Picture puzzles. I. Kresz, Károly. II. Kresz, István. III. Title.

    GV1507.P47K74 2005
    793.73--dc22

                                              2004058952

2 4 6 8 10 9 7 5 3 1

Published by Sterling Publishing Co., Inc.
387 Park Avenue South, New York, NY 10016
Originally published in Hungary under the title *Látványos Fejtörők*
and © 2003 by István Kresz, Károly Kresz, and László Kresz.
English translation © 2005 by Sterling Publishing Co., Inc.
Distributed in Canada by Sterling Publishing
c/o Canadian Manda Group, 165 Dufferin Street
Toronto, Ontario, Canada M6K 3H6
Distributed in Great Britain by Chrysalis Books Group PLC
The Chrysalis Building, Bramley Road, London W10 6SP, England
Distributed in Australia by Capricorn Link (Australia) Pty. Ltd.
P.O. Box 704, Windsor, NSW 2756, Australia

Printed in China
All rights reserved

Sterling ISBN 1-4027-1823-3

CONTENTS

FOREWORD

Logic is an intellectual tool that can connect individuals of all ages. It can span cultures and even languages. Get a group of puzzle fans together and watch them communicate their enthusiasm and share their knowledge—even if they don't speak the same language. And on the subject of a language barrier, this is never more true than between parent and teenager! Logic can go where other tools can't, bringing dialogue, feeling, and pleasure back to the parent-teenager relationship when communication would otherwise be at a standstill.

One of the best tools for developing logic is problem-solving. Solving problems also has another important benefit: Self-awareness. You can learn so much about yourself that you wouldn't otherwise know just by watching yourself at play and by observing the results. You can feel the pleasure and satisfaction of the hero's or heroine's journey as you survey the large, varied, and deep knowledge base you have mastered. As the inventor of Rubik's Cube observed, "There is more intelligence in me than I thought!"

Solving puzzles is intellectual fitness training combined with play: It maintains "mental muscles" while giving pleasure. But in giving pleasure, it does even more. Psychologists have often noted that the brain is the most erotic organ. Thinking is fun. Thinking is pleasure.

Experiments have revealed that human beings produce physiological symptoms very similar to those of sensory pleasure while actively involved in successfully solving a problem. Psychological studies on this subject have demonstrated that the greatest pleasure comes from solving moderately difficult puzzles. Puzzles that are either too difficult or too easy don't result in any real joy or satisfaction.

In this book, relatively easy puzzles have been balanced with relatively hard ones. In other words, every puzzle is "moderately difficult" and can result in extreme pleasure and satisfaction. Just about everyone can solve at least some of these conundrums, and the puzzles are far from being too easy. That's why they're so much fun! Just as important, they're beautiful, both in their intellectual content and their design.

Head-Scratching, Eye-Catching 3-D Conundrums blends modern computer graphics with stimulating puzzles—some of them timeless, historic classics.

New technology has given birth to new ideas and new genres. Three-dimensional computer graphics ushered in a new era in the world of video games—and in the world of puzzles too. This book is part of this new genre—now a recognized, full-fledged genre—and is a treat both for the eye and the mind.

Additionally, this genre is special because it isn't necessary to deface the puzzles by writing on them. They remain clean and solvable even after many years, when they will be every bit as engrossing. It's been two years since I put together my first book. Recently I picked up that volume again and made a fascinating discovery: Solving those puzzles a second time gave me the same joy as it had the first time. I felt the same buzz during the second encounter as I had during my initial one.

Finally, I have one regret. I consider it a shame that when I first solved those puzzles, I failed to write down how long each one took me. If I had, I'd now be able to see where my analytical skills have improved since the first go-round. For this reason, I highly recommend recording your own solving times as you work on these puzzles. That way, when you pick up this book again years from now (as you undoubtedly will), you'll have the added pleasure of being able to outdo yourself. I guarantee you'll pick up these puzzles again. And how can I be so sure? I know it because they are that provocative, that beautiful, and that absorbing.

—László Mérő
Budapest, Hungary

1 Remove three green sticks so that three pieces remain, each containing three red balls.

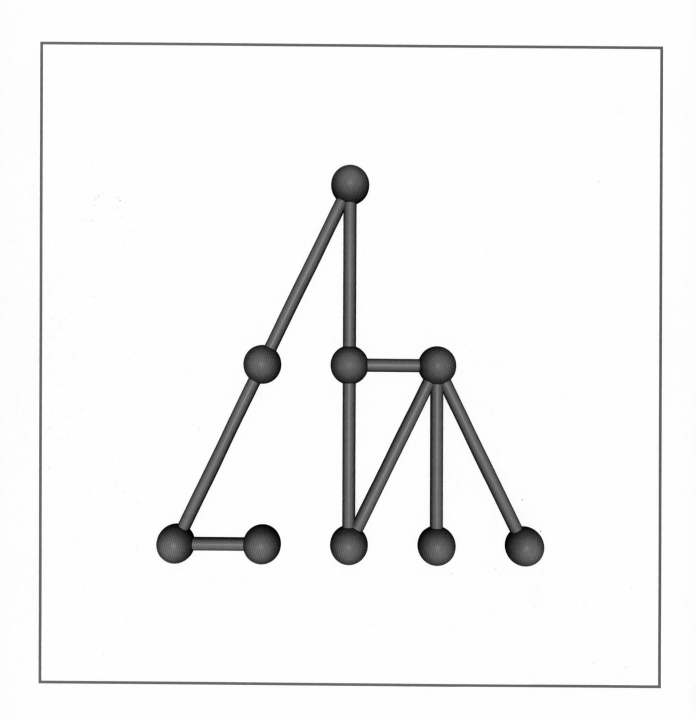

2 Each key has a matching twin except one. Which one is unmatched? (Handles do not need to match.)

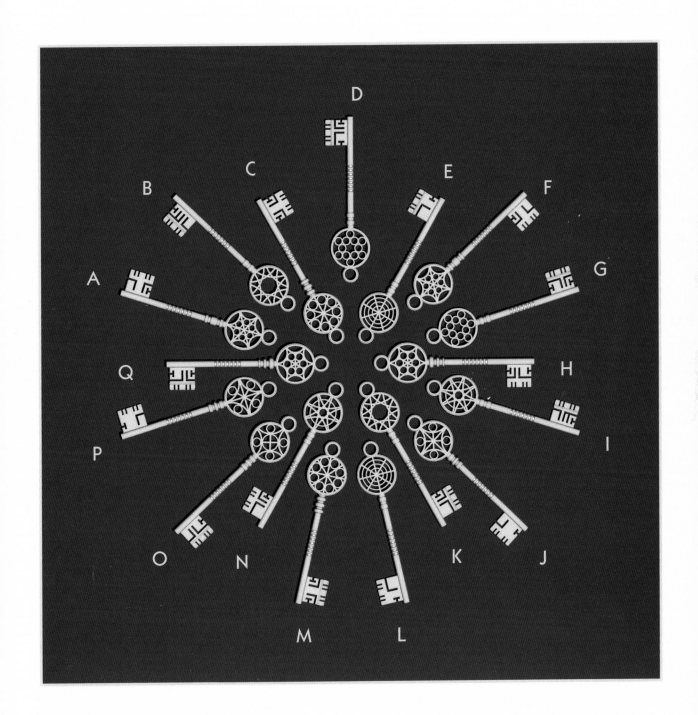

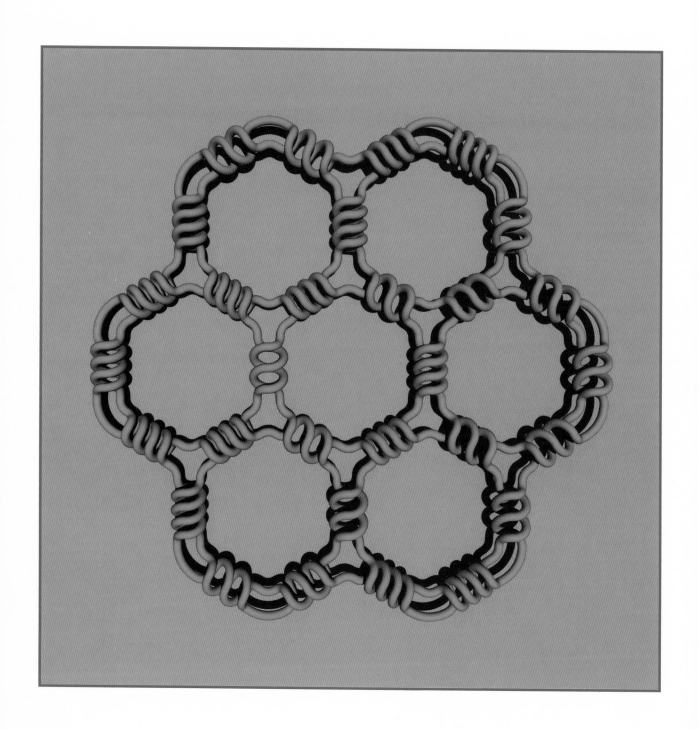

4 In which triangle (defined by three vertices of the hexagon) are there only shapes of different color?

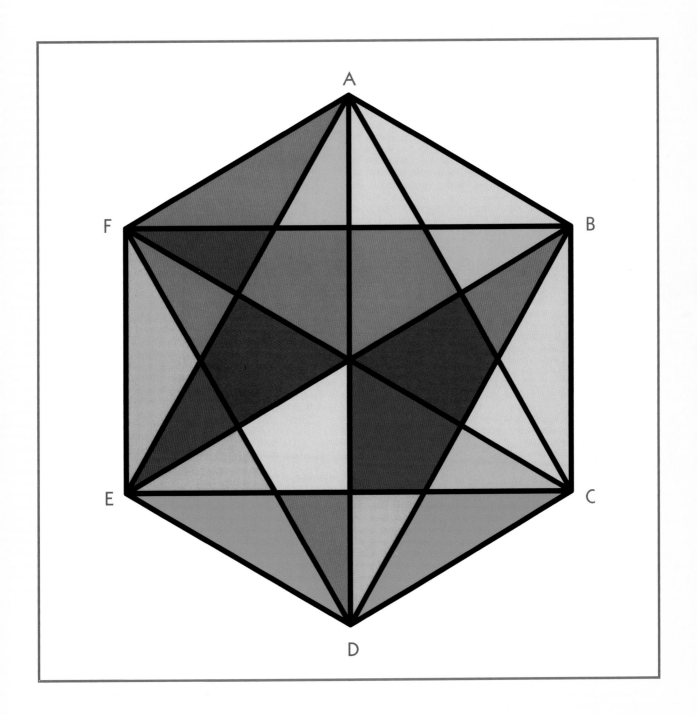

The figure in the middle is the result of placing each of the four surrounding shapes on top of each other. In what order were they placed?

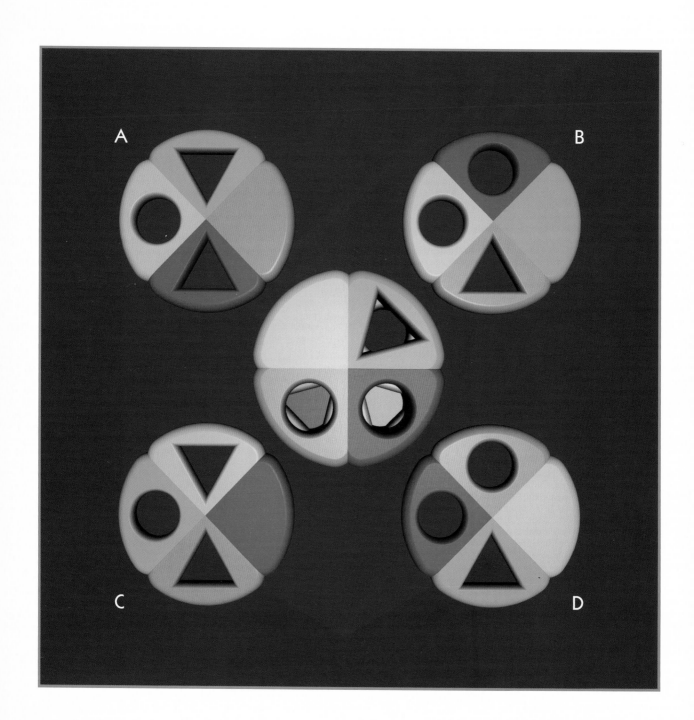

7 The nine vertical green components are held together by horizontal screws. Remove one screw of each color (three altogether) to divide the green block into three parts.

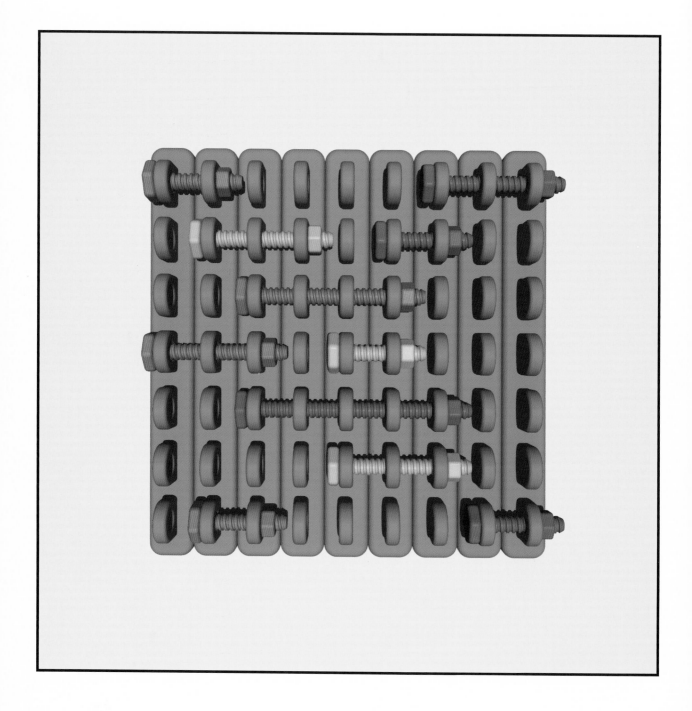

Arrange the four-color shapes in the central box so that the white arrows link areas of the same color.

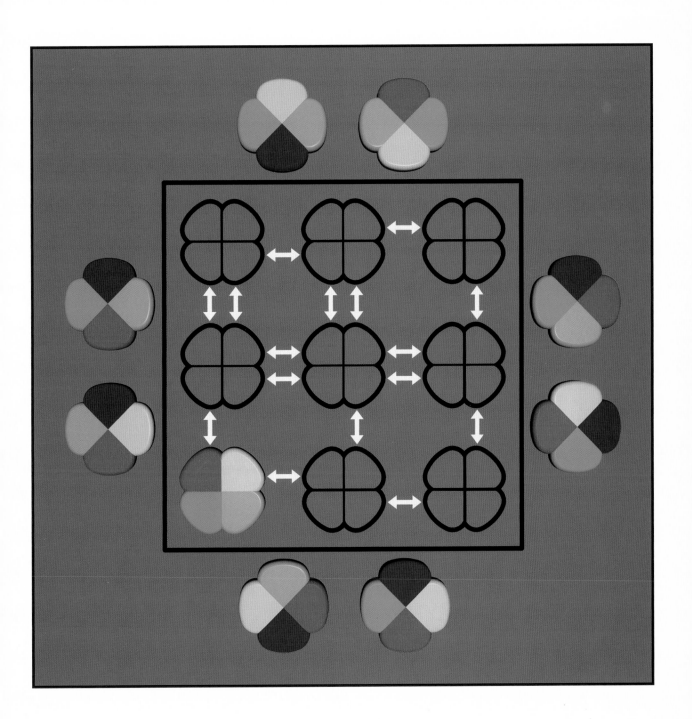

Match the side views of the octopus in the numbered boxes with the top view in the larger, lettered box.

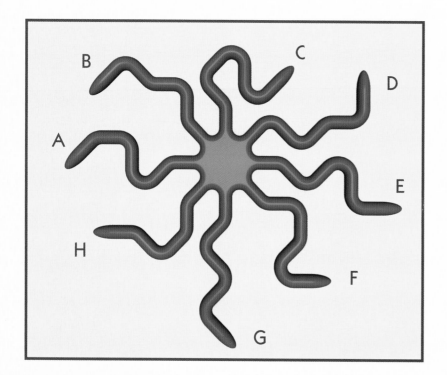

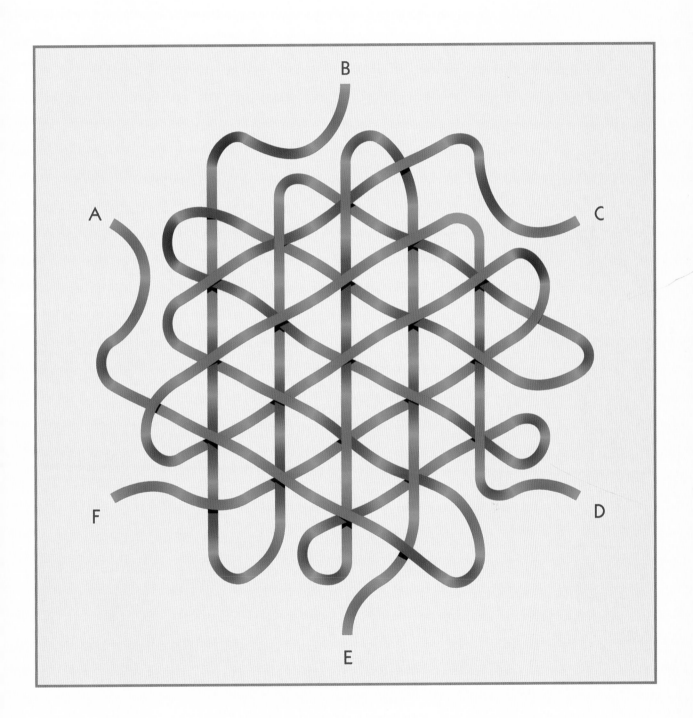

11 Position the four dominoes in the indicated spots so that each colored zigzag area contains the same number of dots.

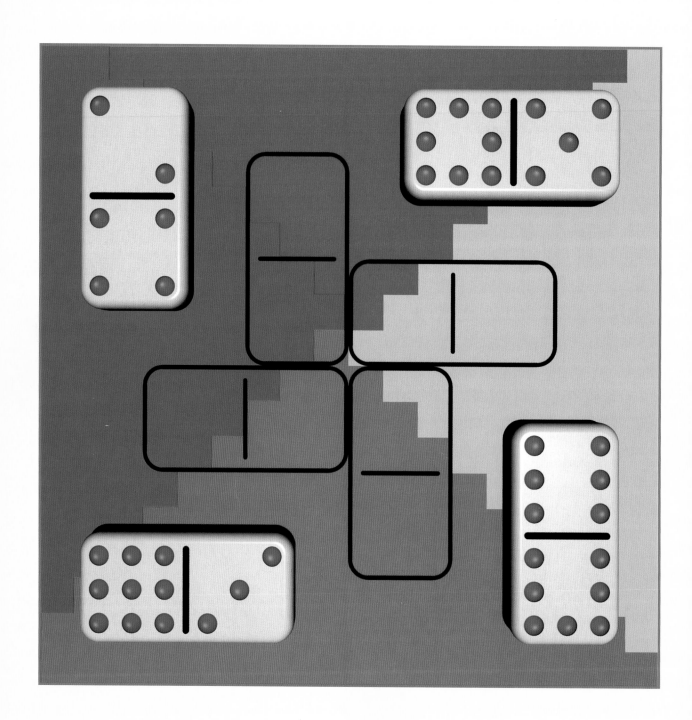

Which two masks are identical?

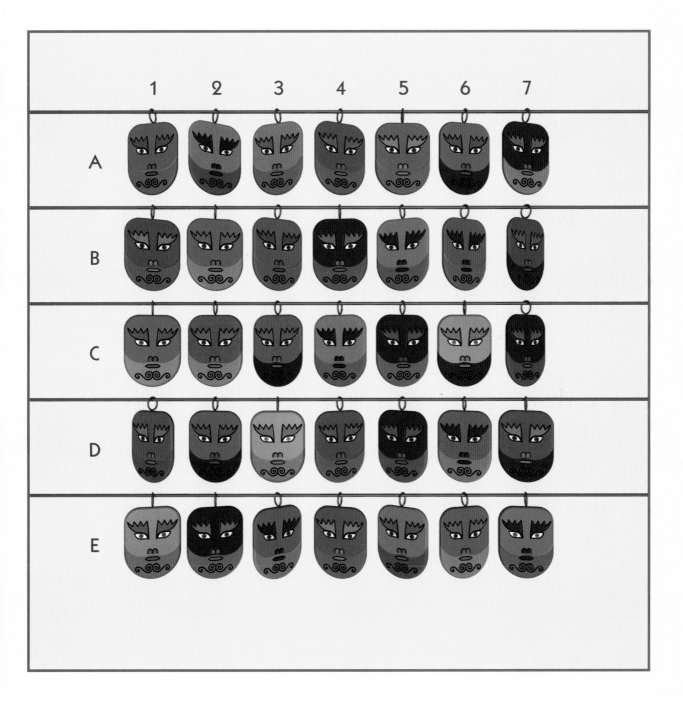

	1	2	3	4	5	6	7
A							
B							
C							
D							
E							

13 The little green monsters at the center of each maze begin eating the candy-coated chocolates at the same time and at the same speed. Which color will have ten pieces eaten first?

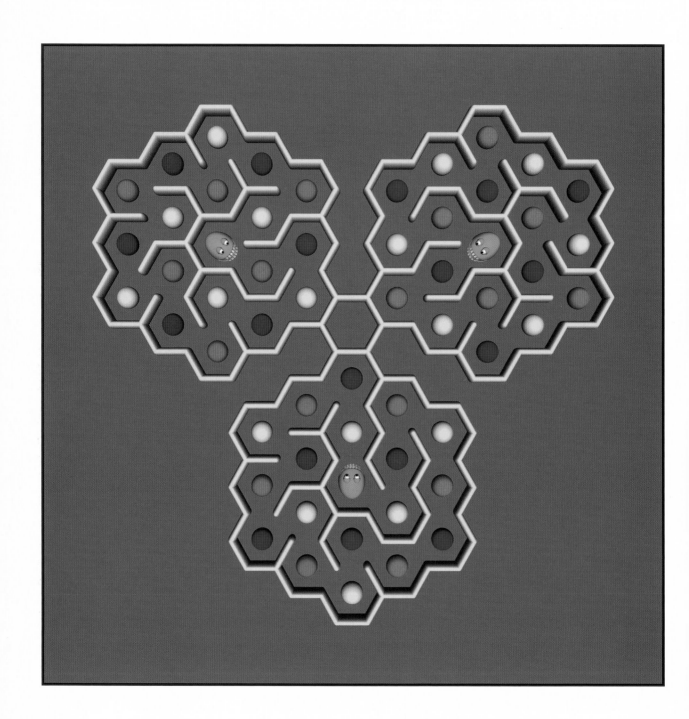

14 Pair each set of five rings with a second set that is linked identically.

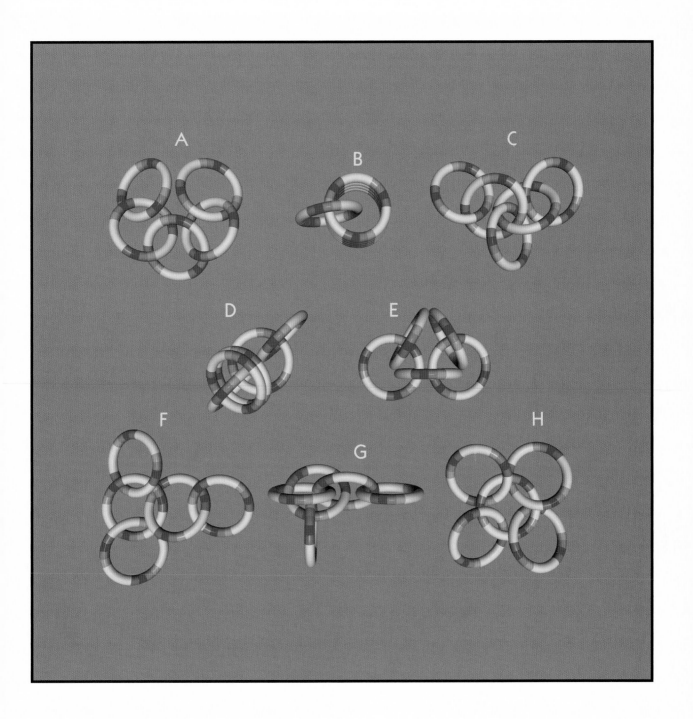

The three 3-D shapes at the bottom of this picture are also shown unfolded. Match them up.

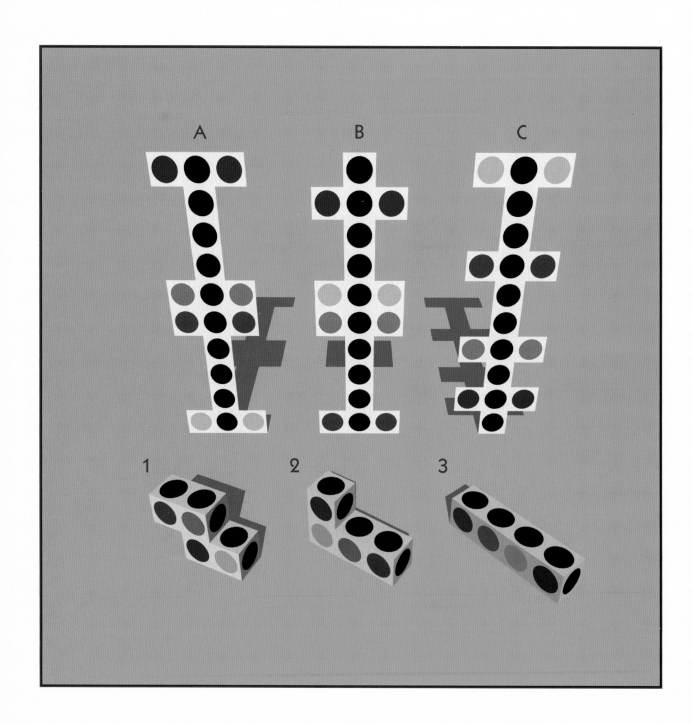

16 Place the six marbles in the labyrinth so that the green row has as many marbles as possible, and so that when you travel along the labyrinth path, you encounter a marble at the same regular interval throughout.

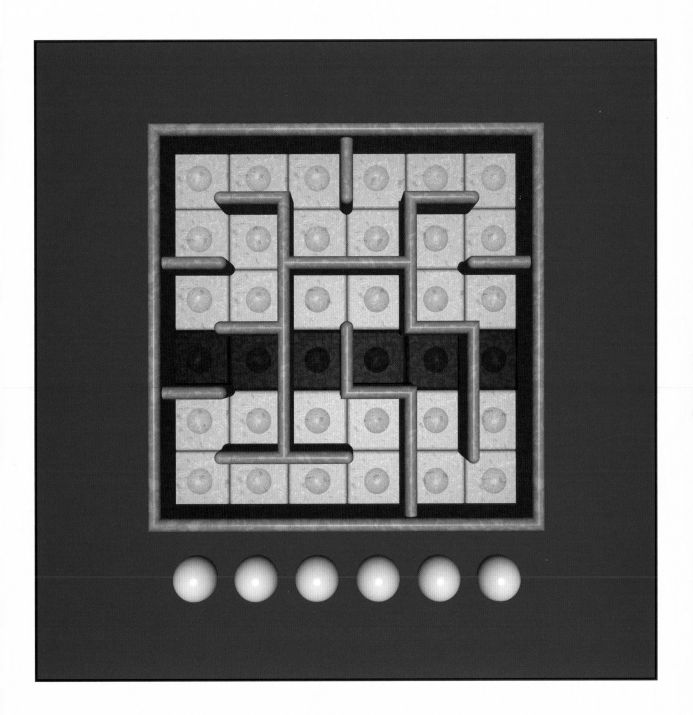

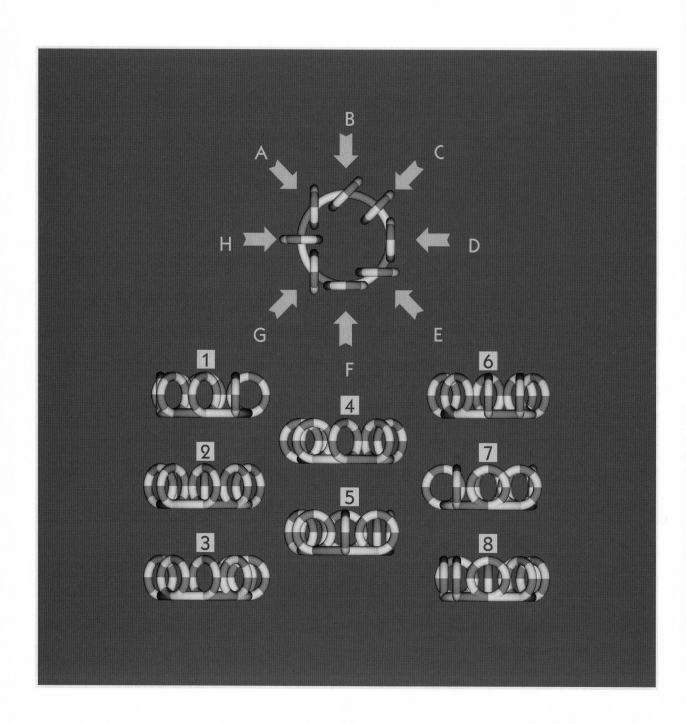

If you turn the wheels of the cog, will the large yellow wheels in the lower left and the top right corners turn in the same or opposite directions?

Match the words with the eight figures. The first figure is shown in three colors as an example.

Match the figures that contain the same shapes.

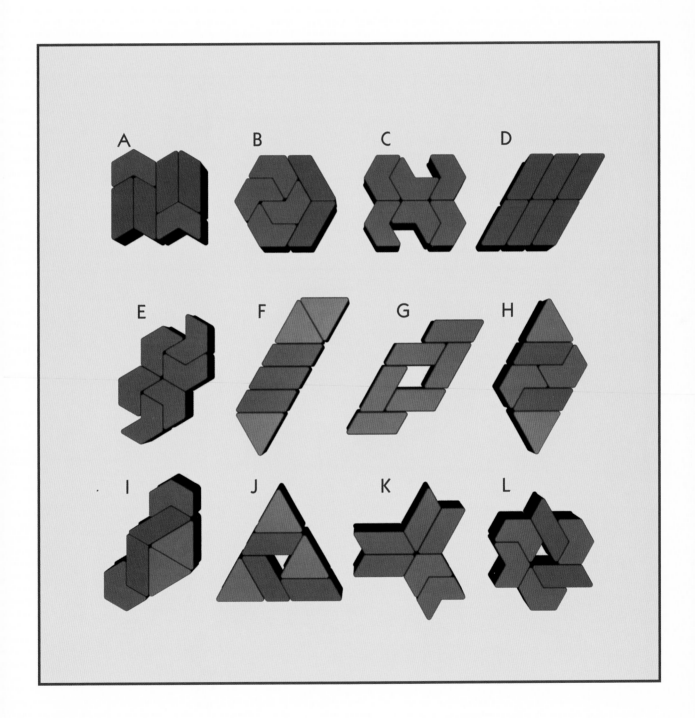

21 Which of the four outer designs is shown upside down in the center?

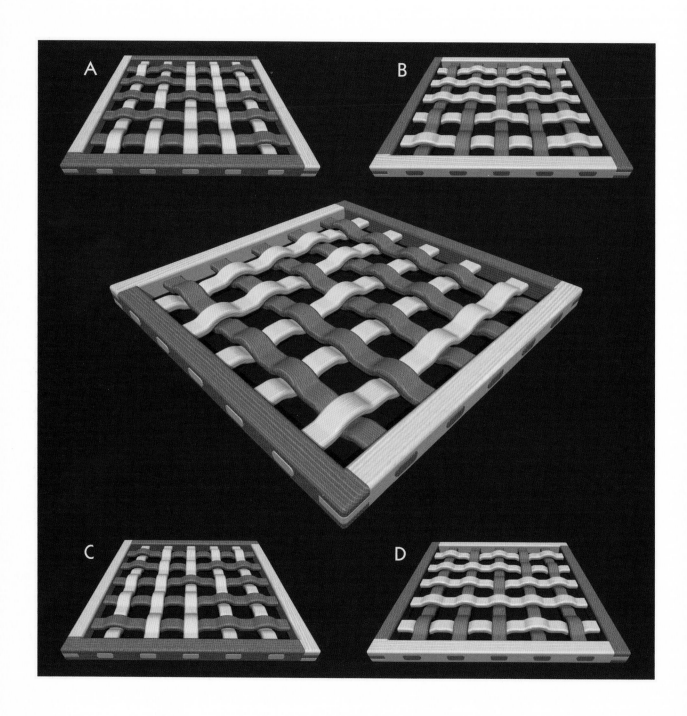

22 Cover the six-by-six checkerboard in the center with the wooden shapes that surround it. The holes must be placed where the checkers are.

The structure at the bottom was created from the pieces at the top. Pair up the numbered and lettered pieces.

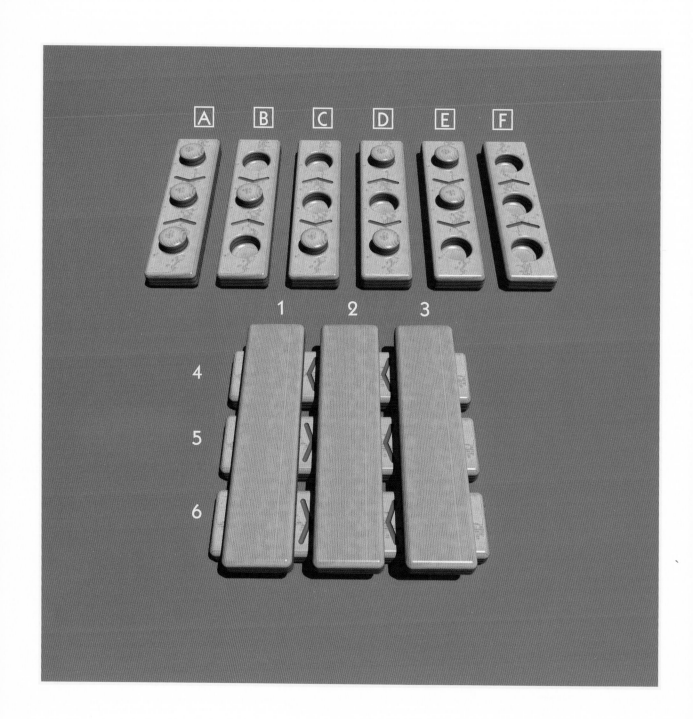

Place the colored shapes on the grid so that adjacent parts are the same color.

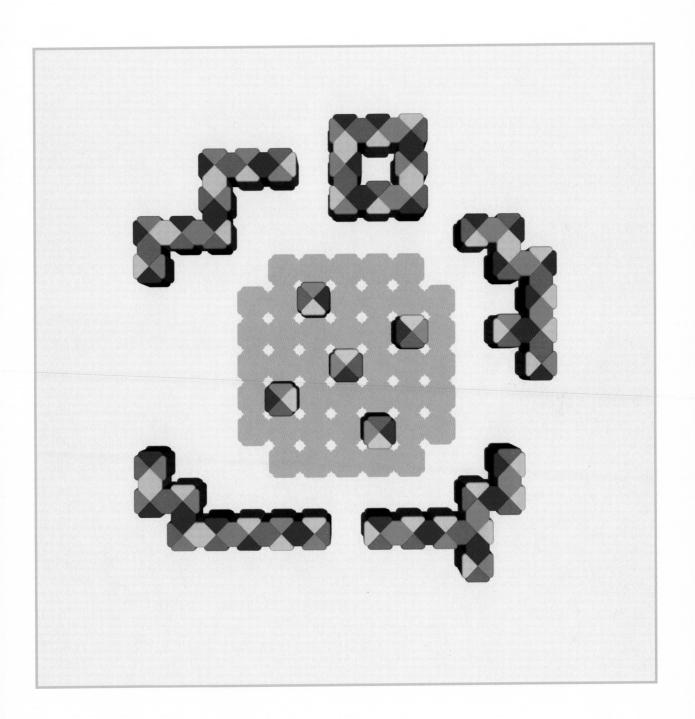

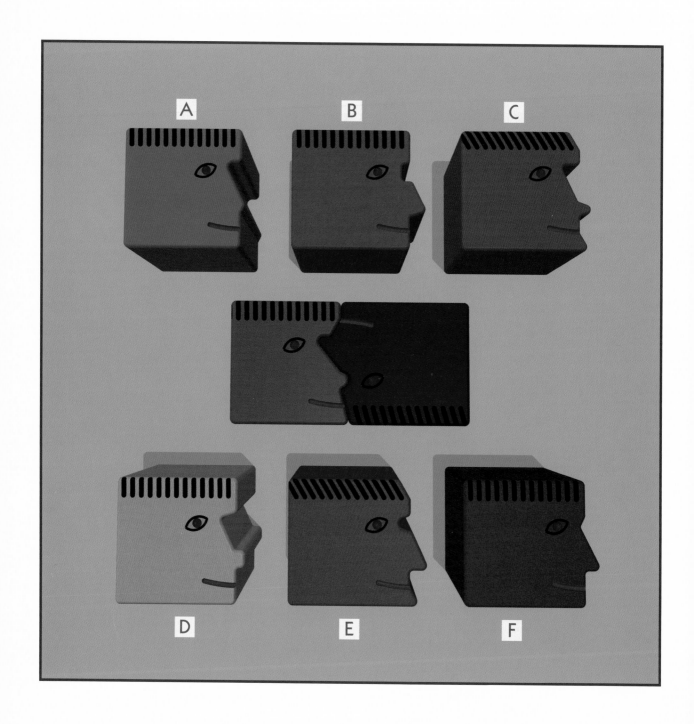

Place the five wooden pieces (A through E) in the spots
(1 through 5) to complete the jigsaw.

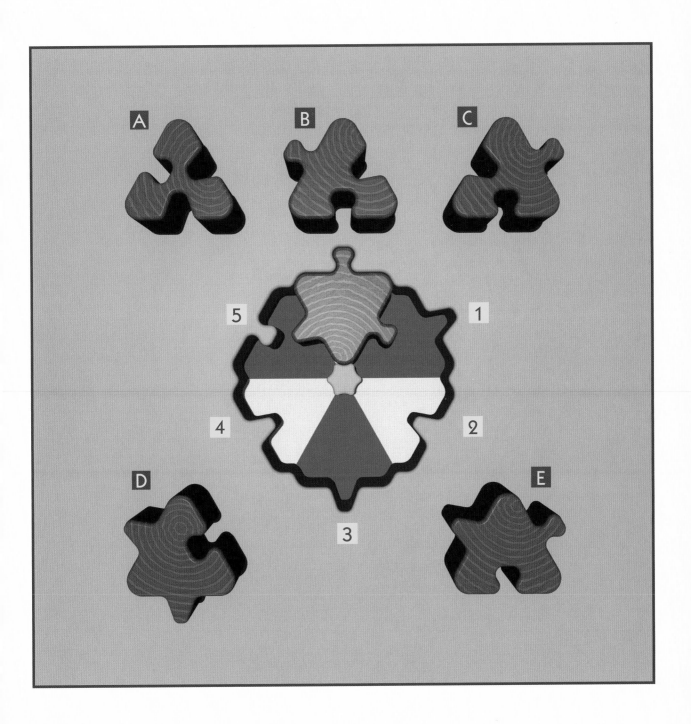

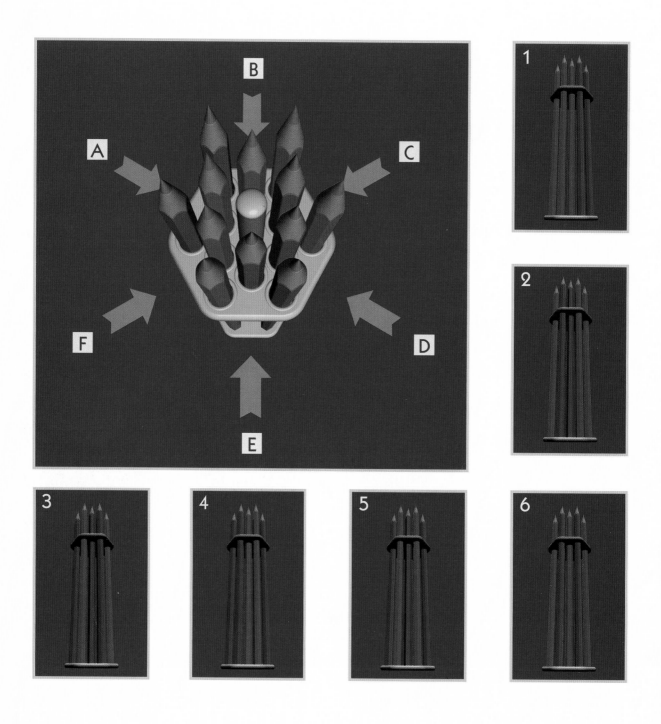

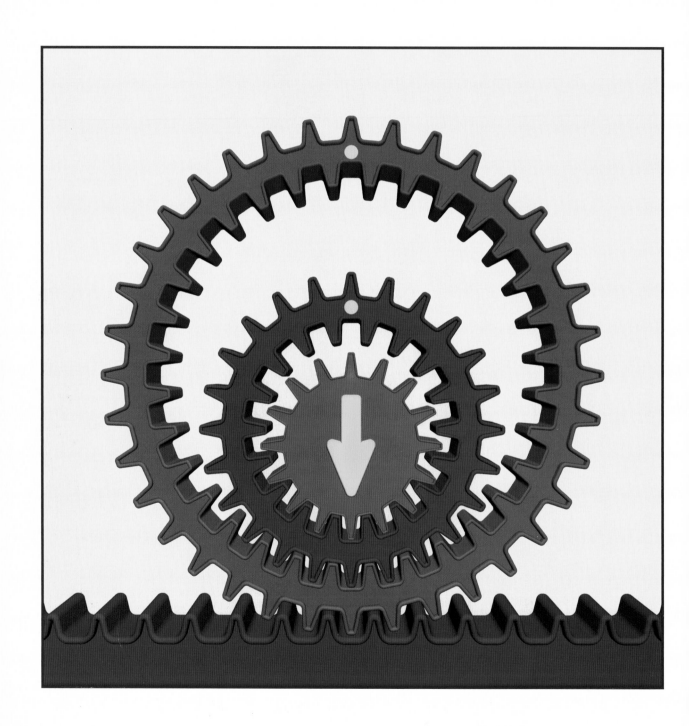

30 Can you find the way to attach the four outside wedges to the center one to create a complete cheese wheel?

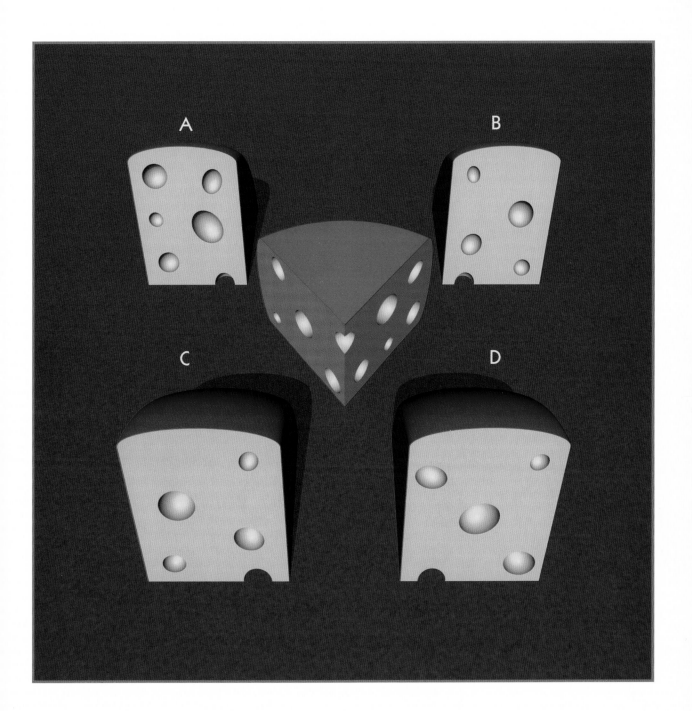

The numbered shapes are made from the lettered columns of paper. Can you pair them up correctly?

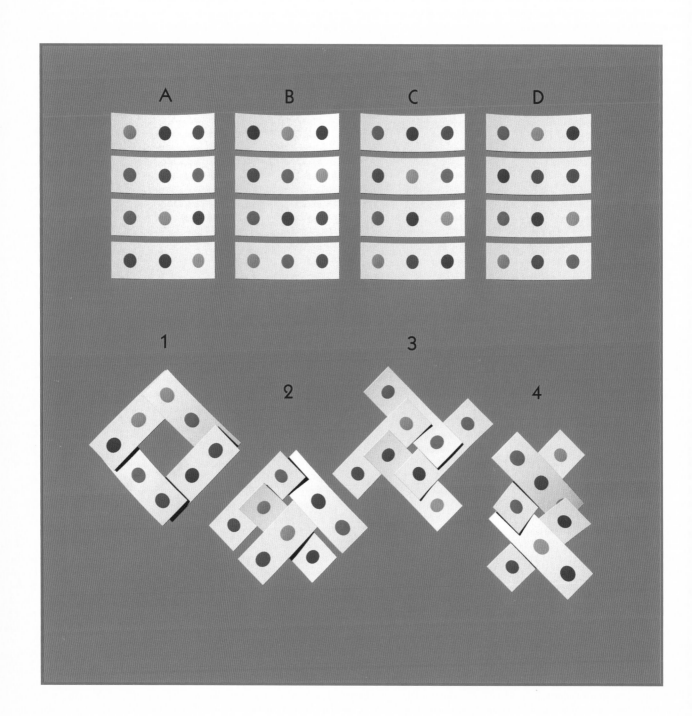

32 How many knots will form on the string if you pull the ends in opposite directions?

Place the tied shape into its container in such a way that neither the columns nor the rows contain two rings of the same color.

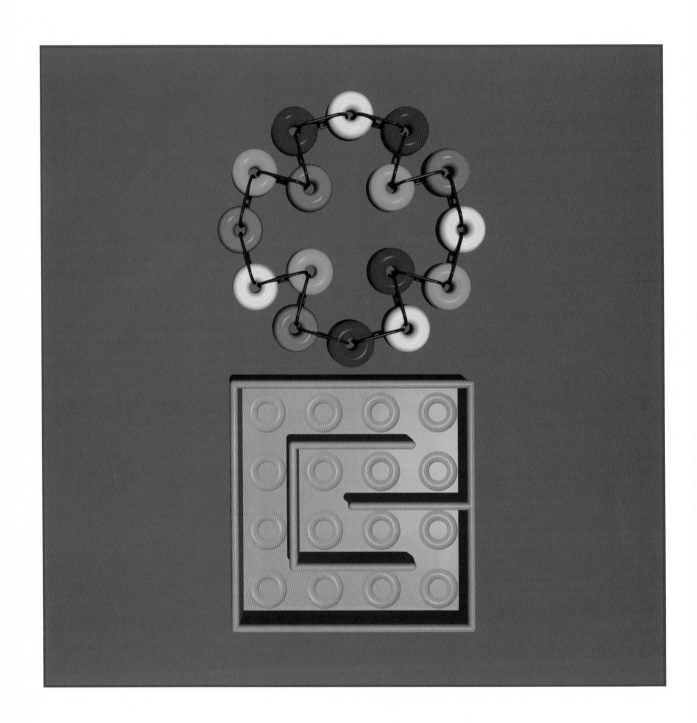

34 The numbered figure shows the top view of four dice. The lettered figures, each showing three dice, are the side views from each arrow. Match the lettered figures with the numbered arrows. All are standard dice with opposite sides adding up to 7.

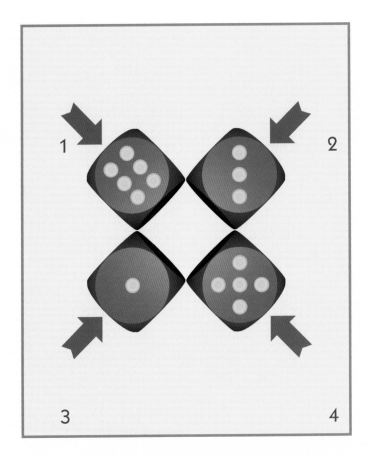

1

2

3

4

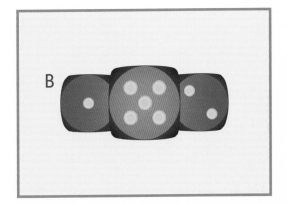

B

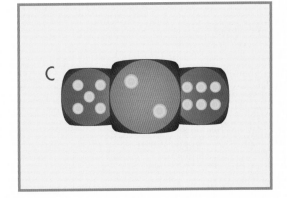

C

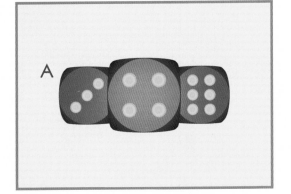

A

D

Place the columns on the bases so no two windows are at the same level.

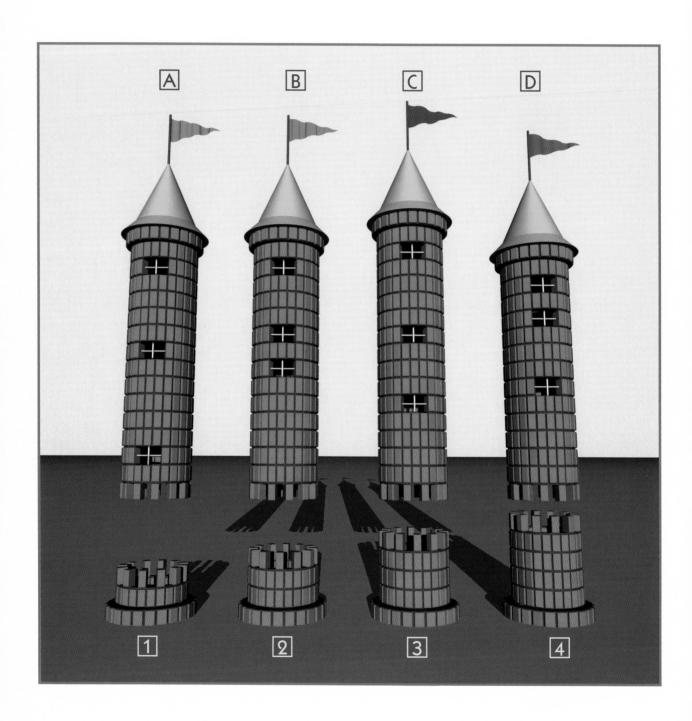

36 Place the arrows on the grid so each number is pointed to by that many arrows.

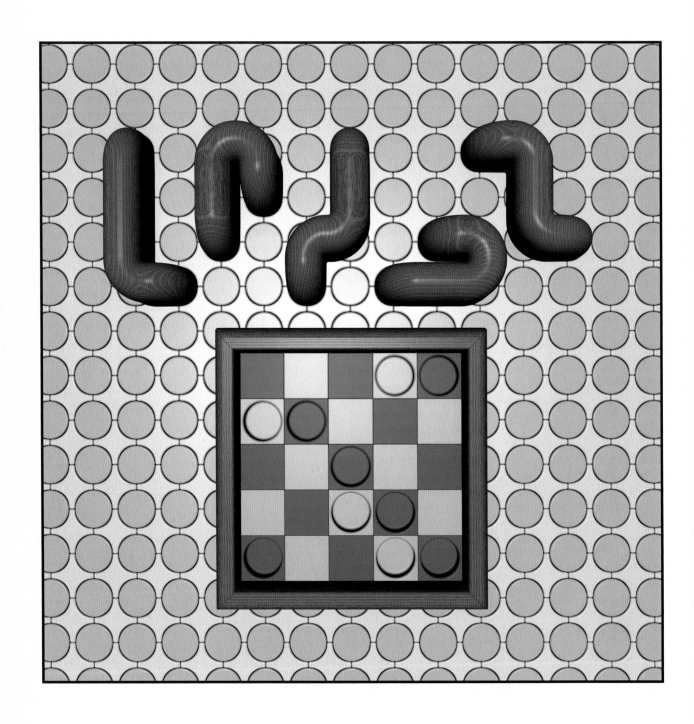

Following the rules of dominoes, replace the blank tiles in the center with dominoes from one of the four sets surrounding it. You may use only one color and must use all nine tiles of that color.

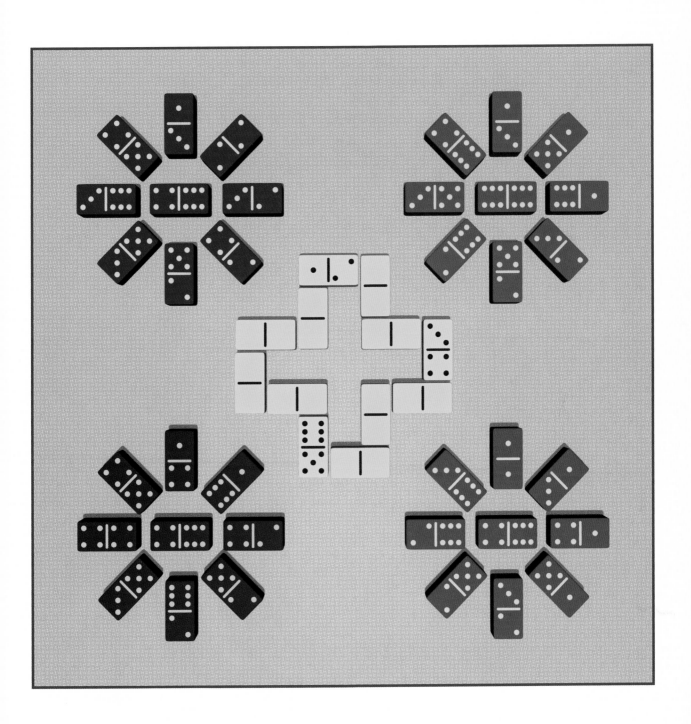

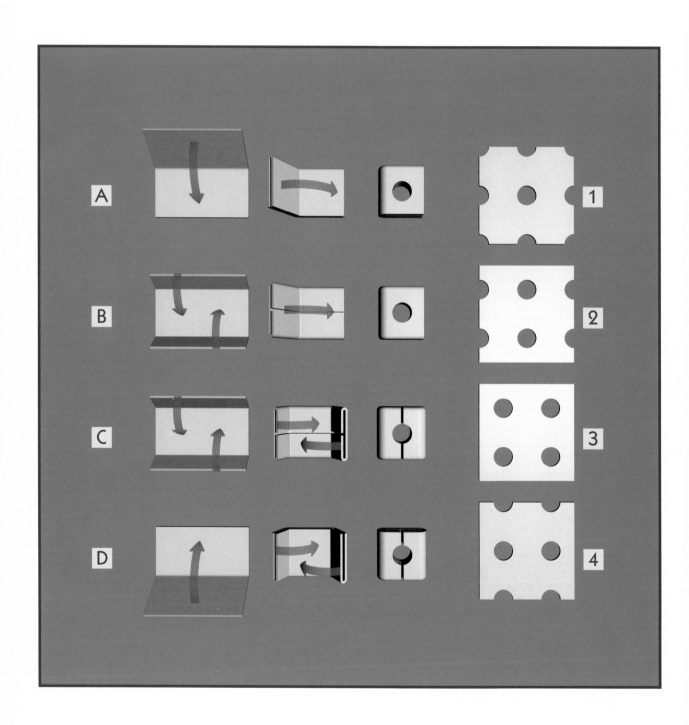

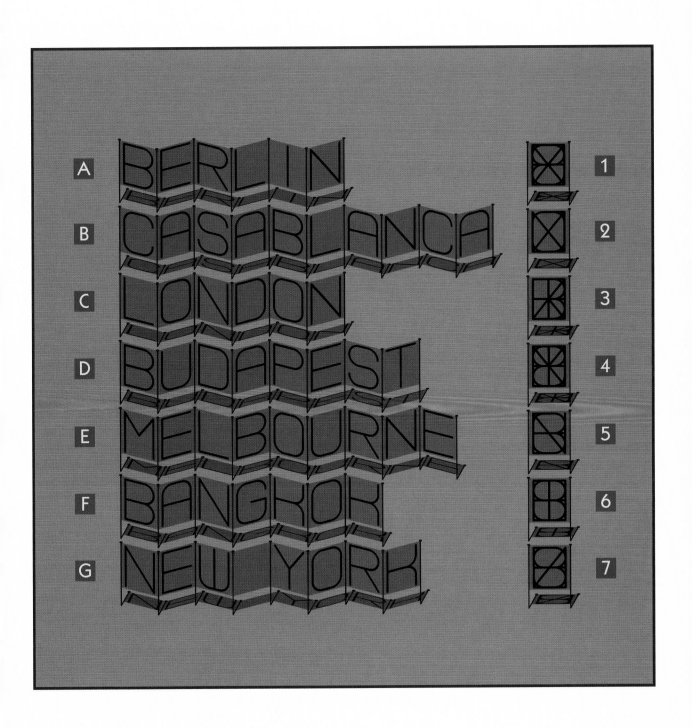

Rearrange the green segments so that all the arrows point to a bull's-eye.

Rearrange the shapes so that each of the six equations from blue circle to blue circle is correct.

In what order have the five pieces been placed on top of one another to create the center shape?

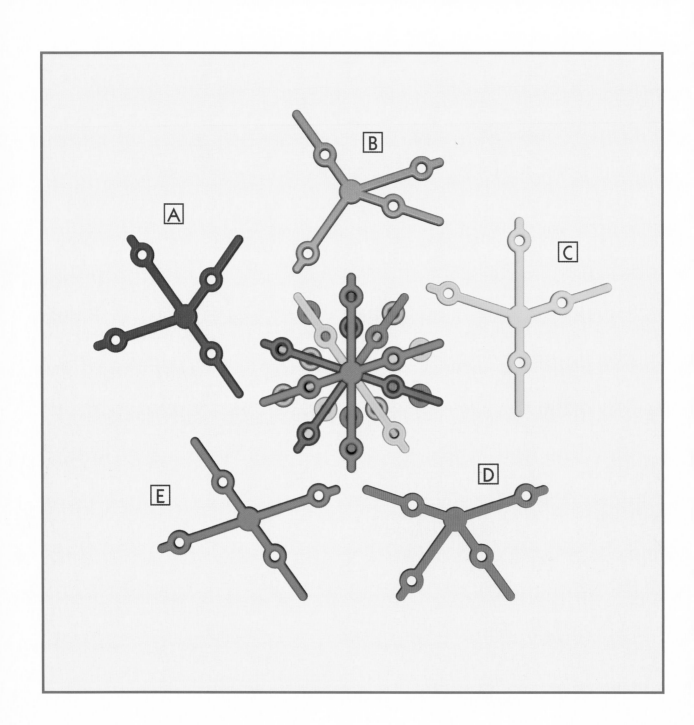

The lumberjacks are cutting the branches from under each other. The number in white is the time it takes to saw that branch off. How many lumberjacks will manage to remain on their branch?

Match the endpoints of the shapes and determine the order in which they were placed upon each other.

Form four hearts (congruent with the one in the center) from the twelve lettered pieces. Pieces may be flipped.

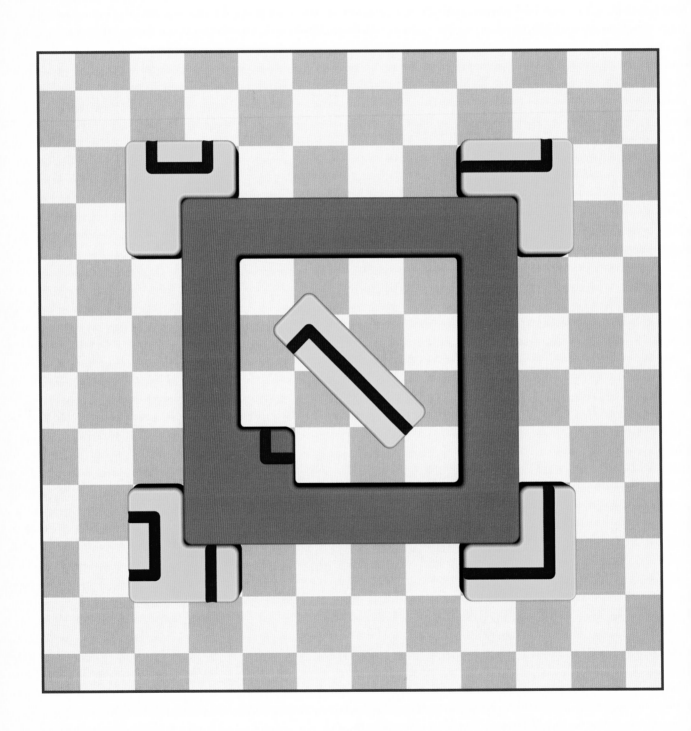

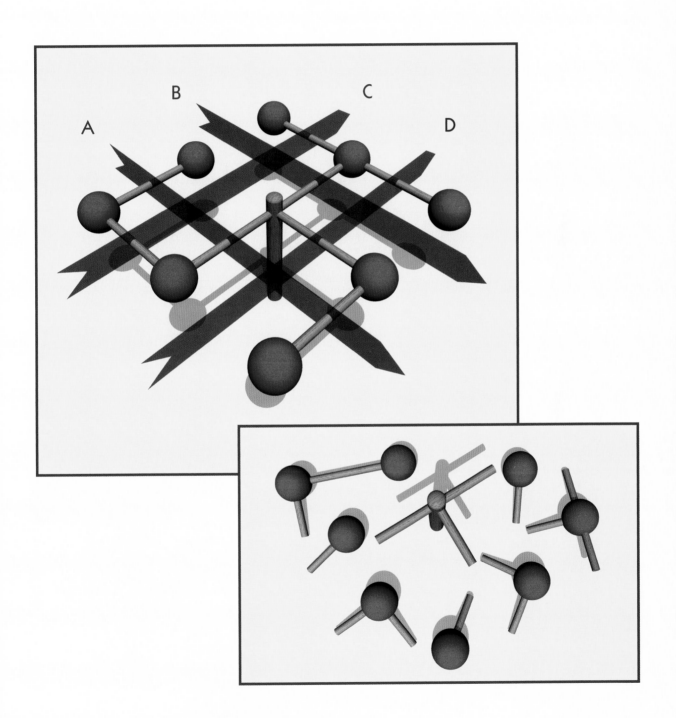

49 Pair up the side and top views.

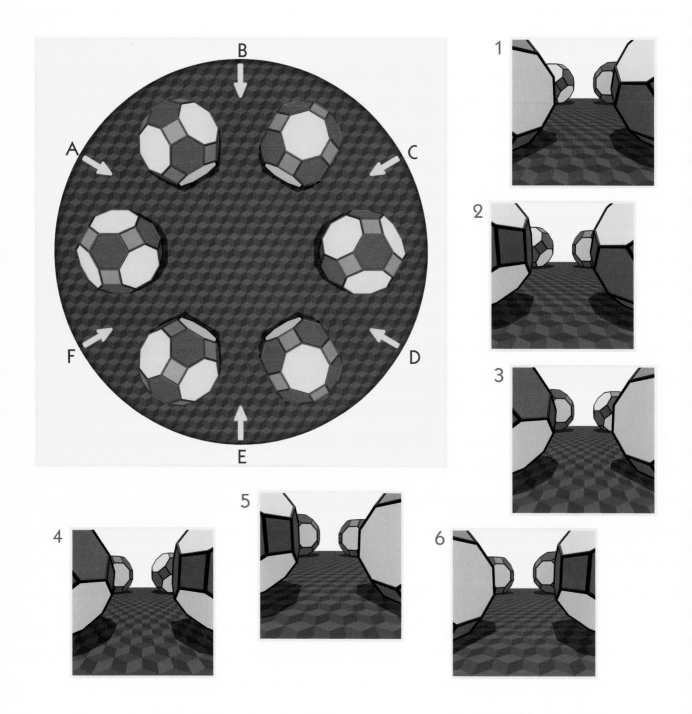

Where do you exit the labyrinth if you begin at the arrow on the bottom of the figure? Turning around is not permitted. Every time you step on a yellow, blue, or green square, the arrow blocks of that color slide one square to the left or right.

The red lines on the yellow disk cut its perimeter into fourteen pieces of the same length. How many one-fourteenth turns will it take to rotate the disk until the red line forms a continuous loop?

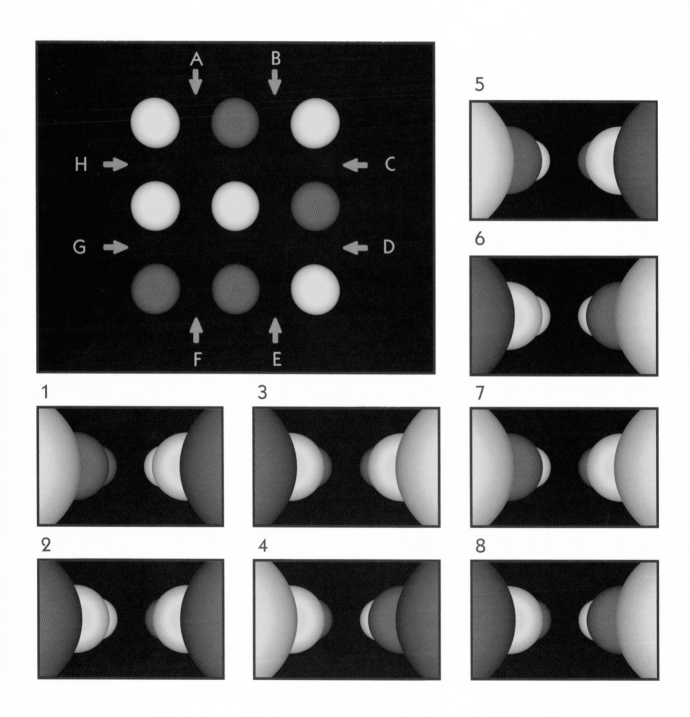

54 Pair up the ends of each ribbon.

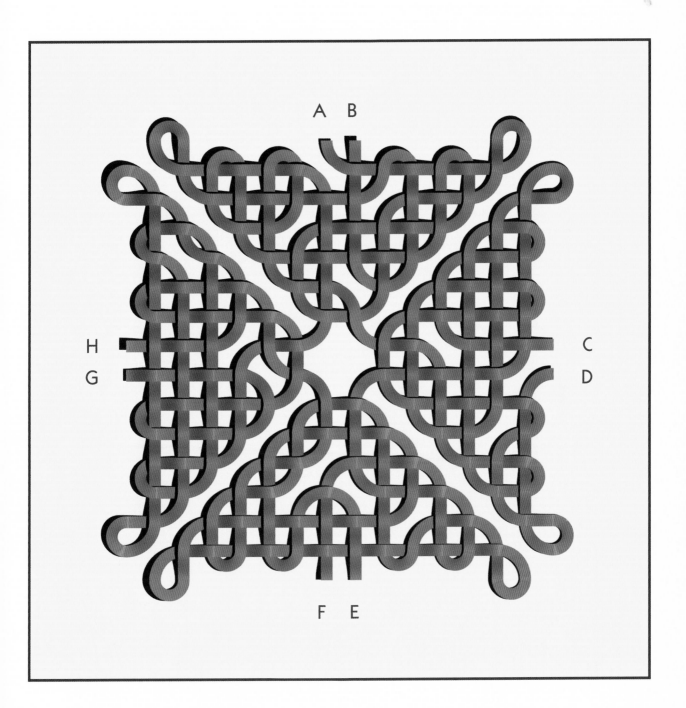

55 Using the stand components on the left (without the flower-pots), assemble a plant stand for the potted plants on the right.

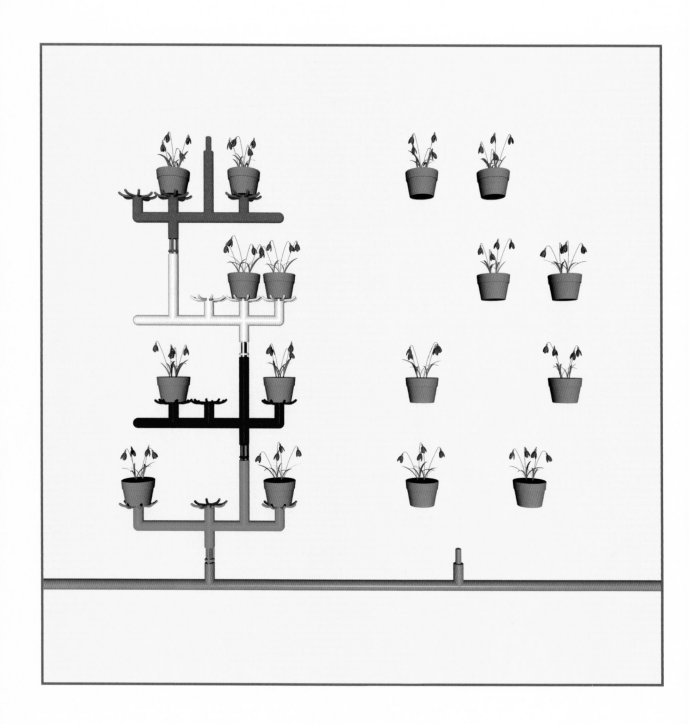

In what order can all the shapes be pushed into the box?

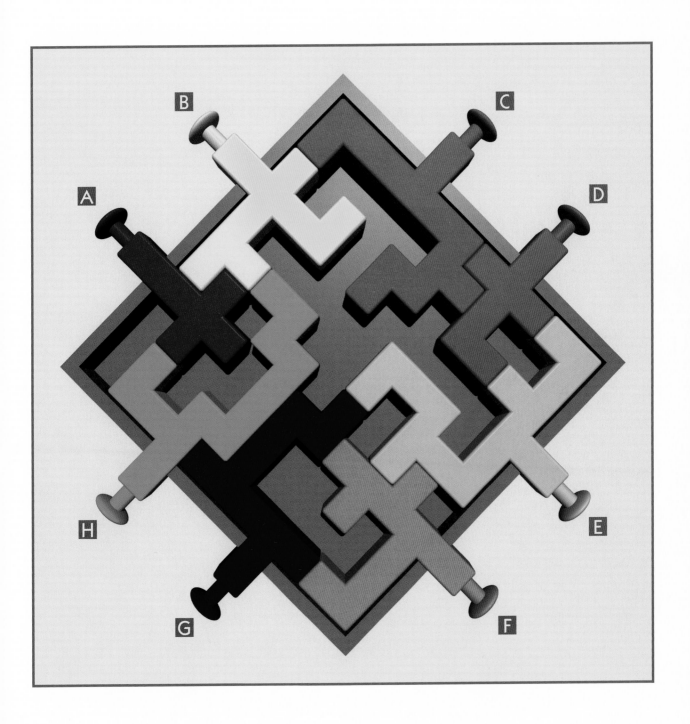

57 Place the numbers 1 through 7 on the green spheres so that the number inside each triangle equals the sum of the numbers on its corners.

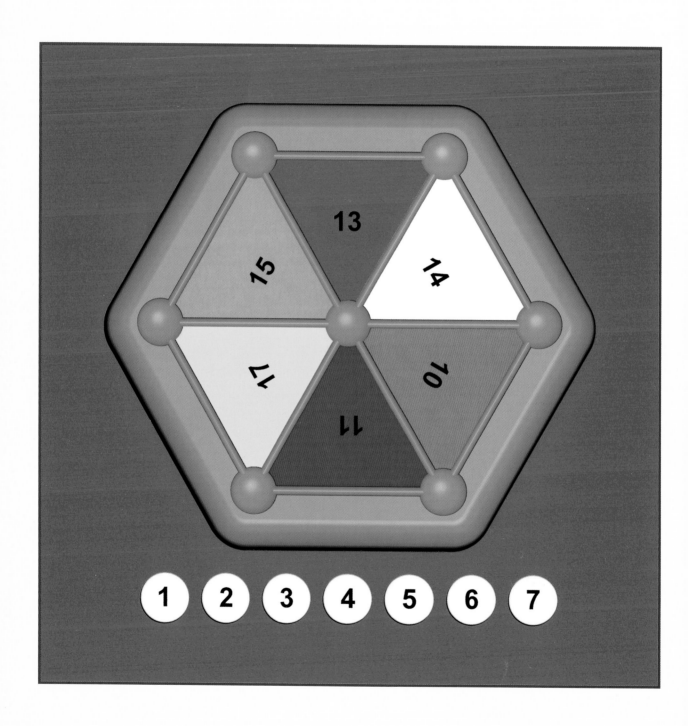

58 Each tub is marked with the number of gallons of water it holds. Water flows at the same rate from each tap. Which color taps should all be opened so that the same amount of water flows into the bottom two tubs?

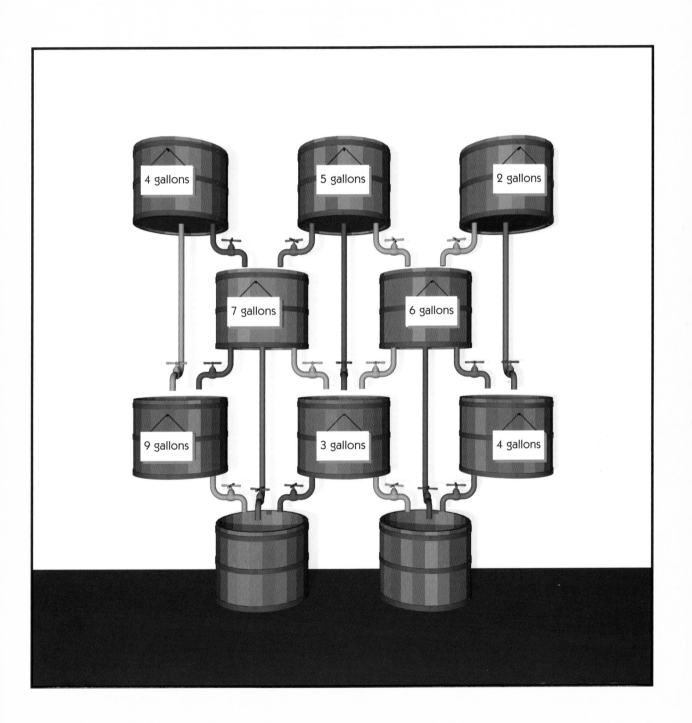

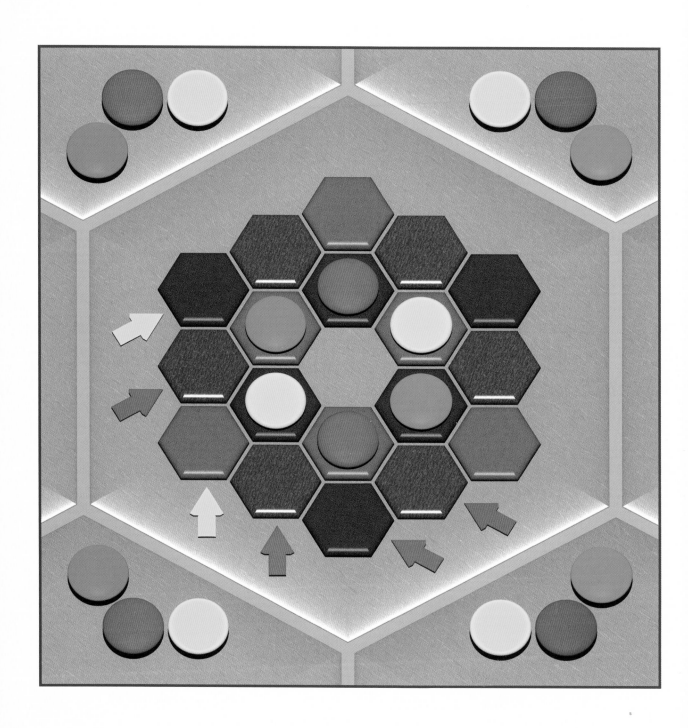

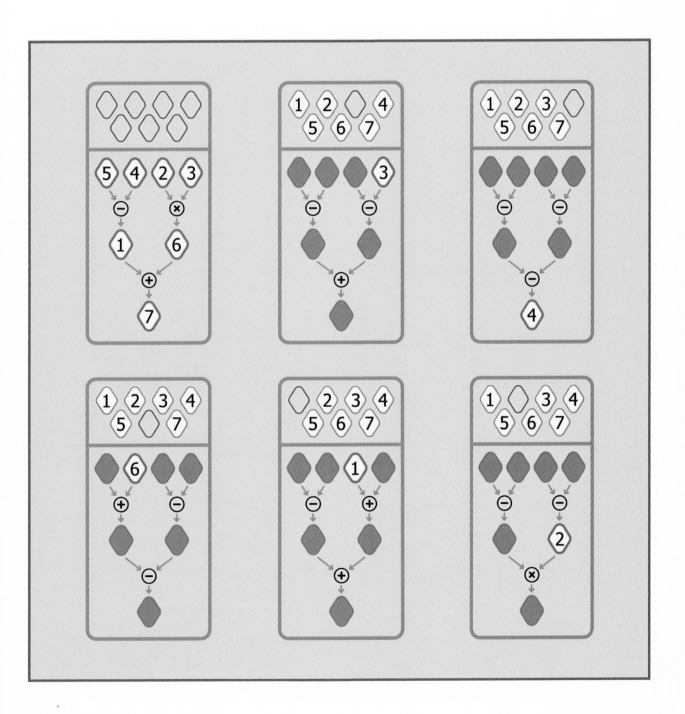

Place the green shapes on the grid so that three identical signs are *not* next to each other either vertically, horizontally, or diagonally.

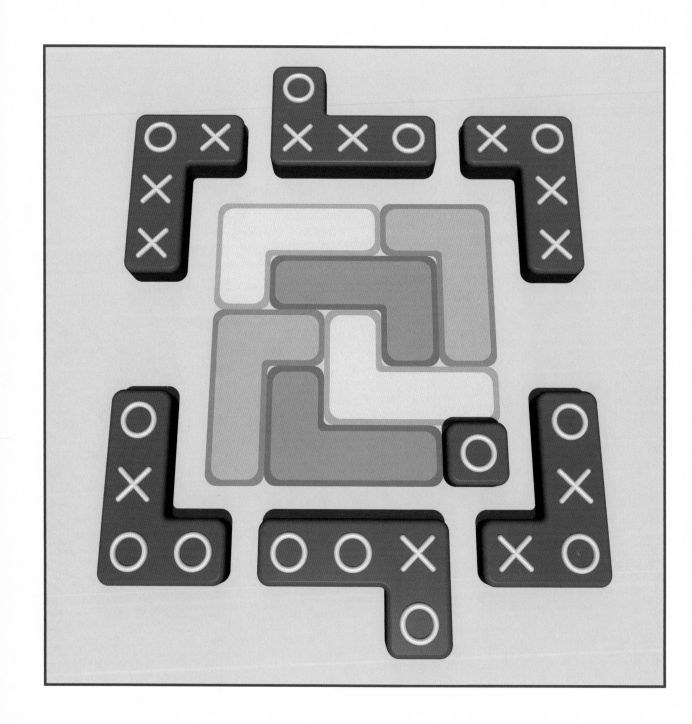

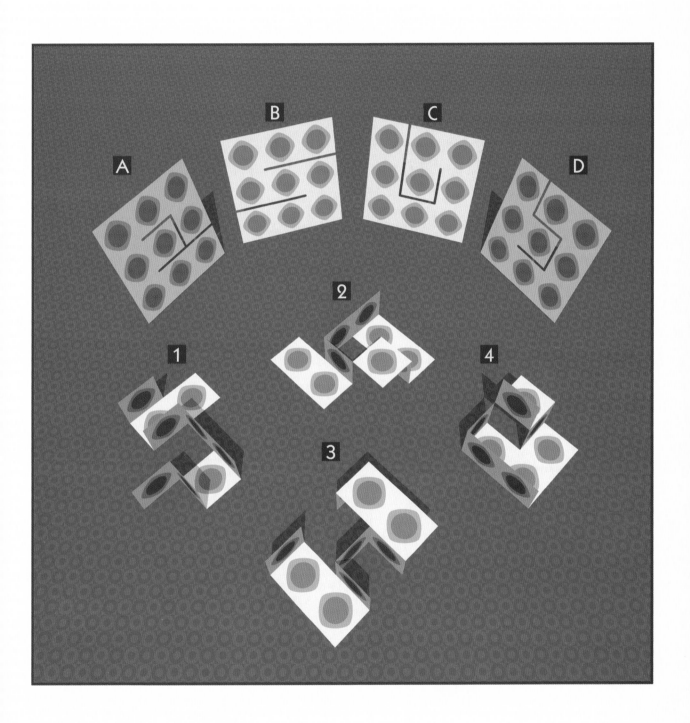

64

The different-color weights weigh 1, 2, 3, 4, and 5 pounds, respectively. Weights of the same color weigh the same. What does each color weigh?

65 Pair up the lettered side views of the plants with the numbered arrows in the top view.

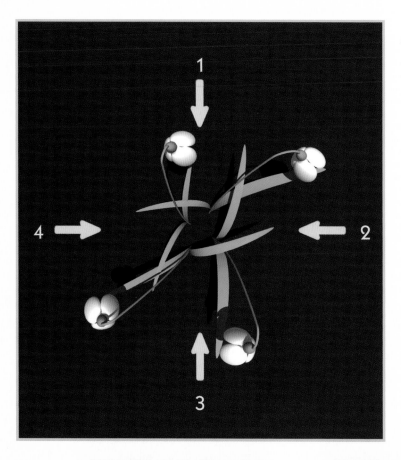

A

B

C

D

66 Which of the four drawings shows the top view of the three tricycles?

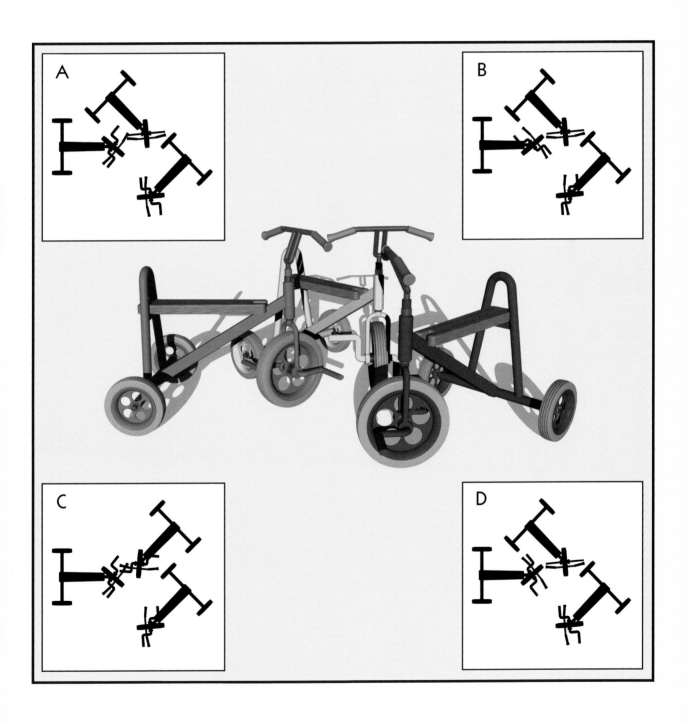

In what order do the green balls fall out of the yellow mazes, if they spin at identical speeds in the direction indicated by the arrows?

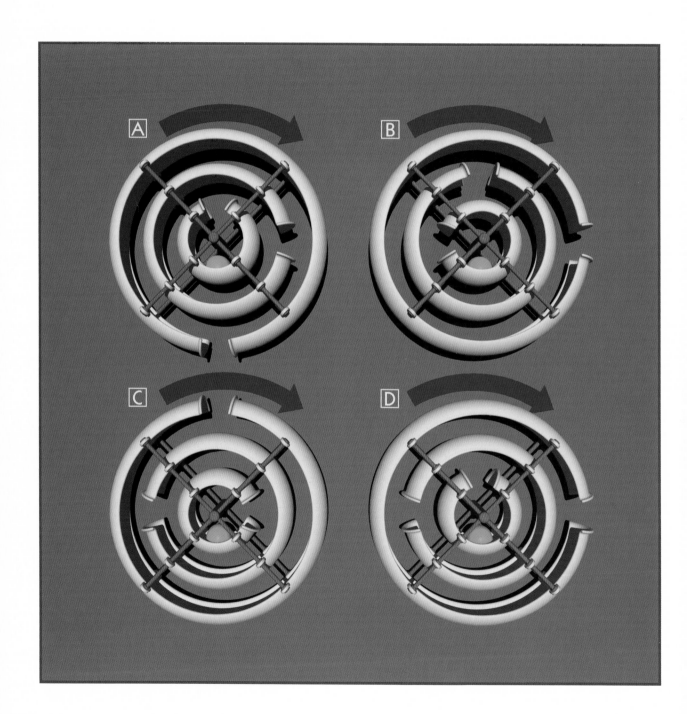

Place the eight soccer balls onto the eight holders. Both colors of each soccer ball must be on its holder.

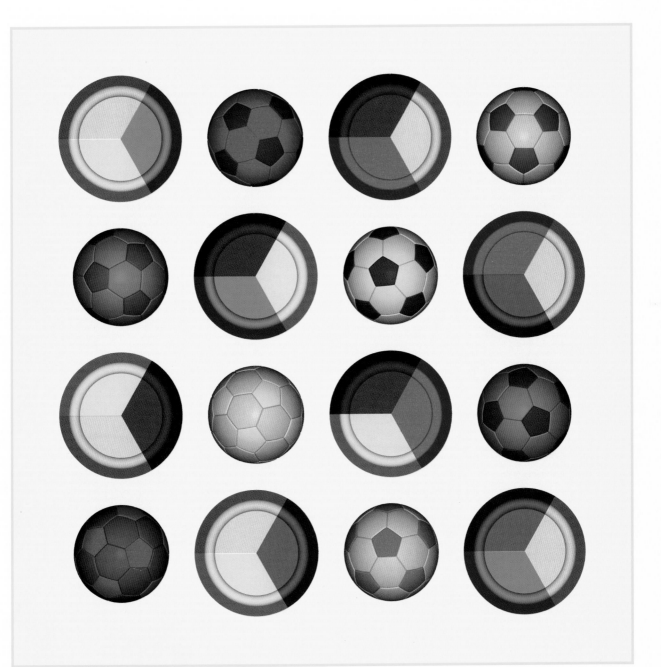

Place the numbers in the septagon so that the sum of any four numbers in a row is 30.

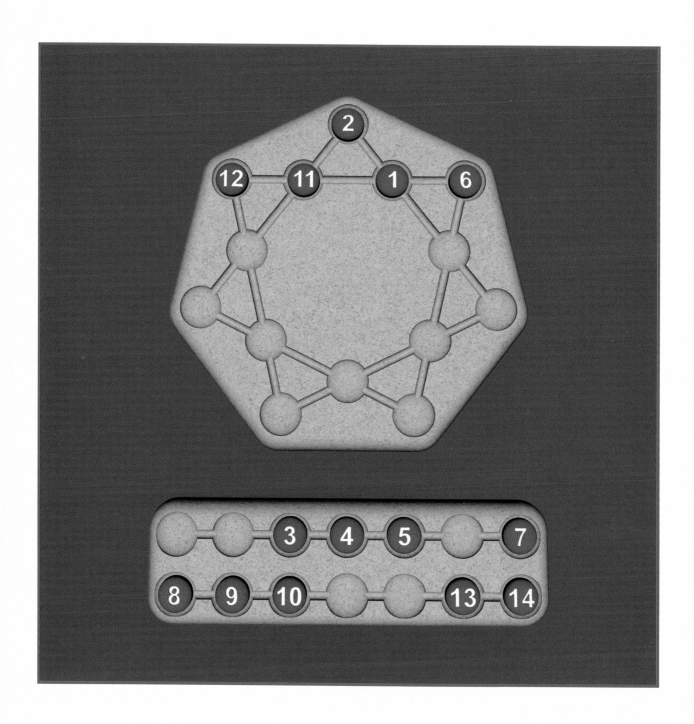

70 Three identical dice were joined together. The numbers on the sides joined match. Which of the four side views is correct? All are standard dice with opposite sides adding up to 7.

A

B

C

D

How many balls will end up in each goal if all twelve are rolled one after the other in the direction indicated by its arrow?

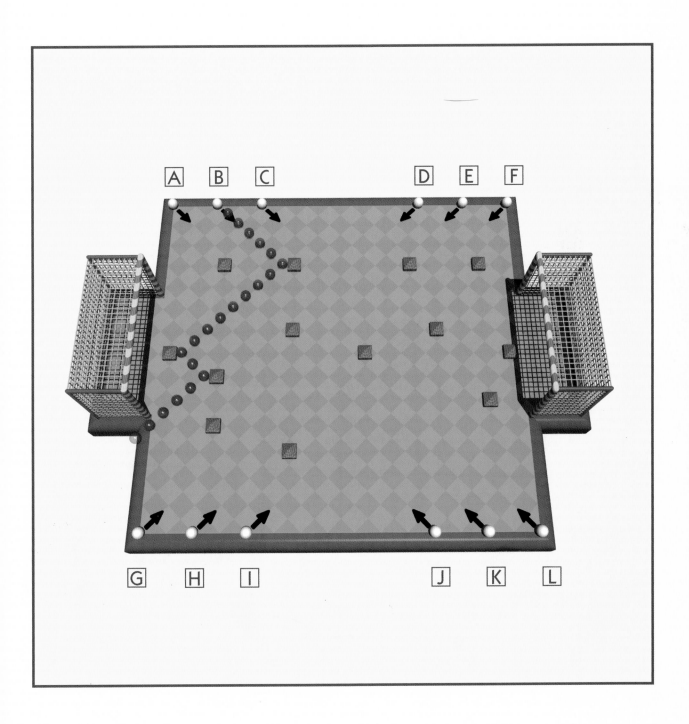

The three small pictures show how different-color robots throw a ball. How many passes will it take to get the ball into the basket, and which robot will succeed at it?

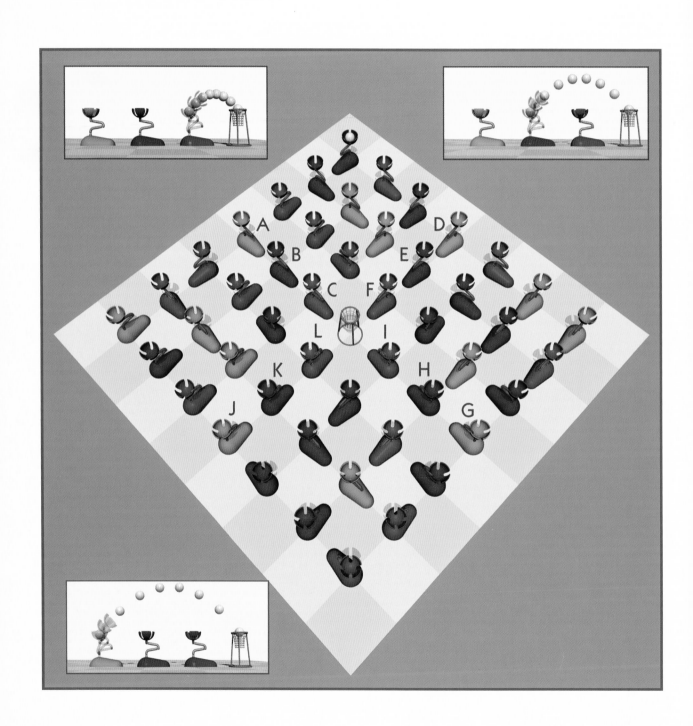

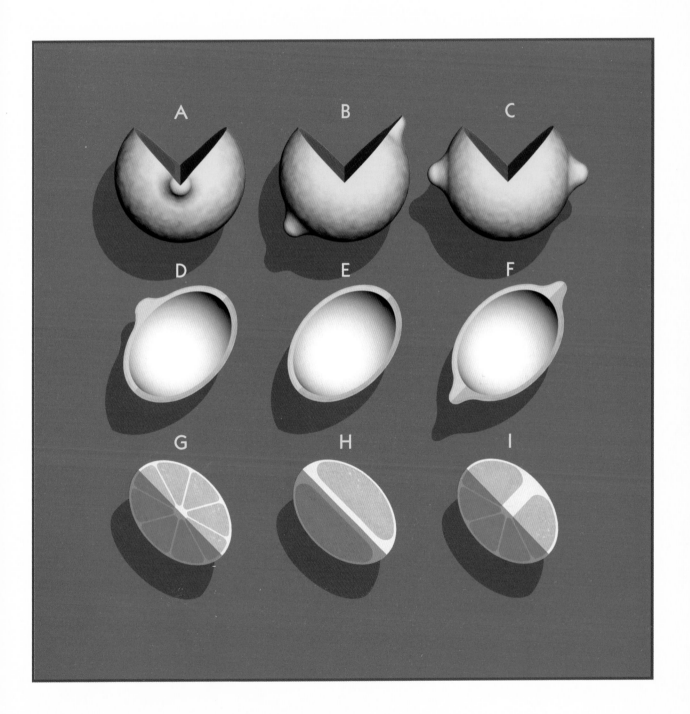

In what order should the pebbles be shot from the slingshot to deflate every balloon?

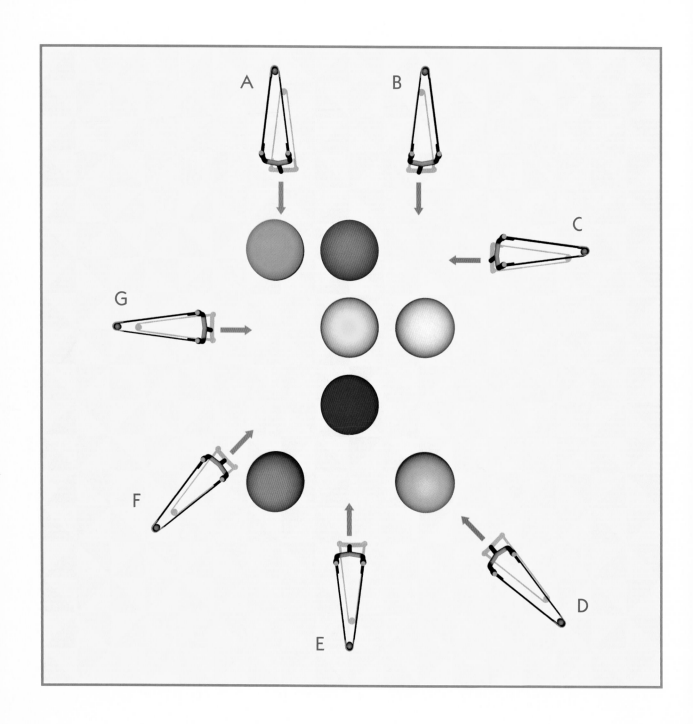

76 Place the cubes onto the yellow grid so that the sum of the numbers in each row, column, and central diagonal is the same.

Pair up the matching balloons whose designs are symmetrical. Which one is left?

78 Move one card from each of the sets of five cards so that the sum of the numbers in each set is identical.

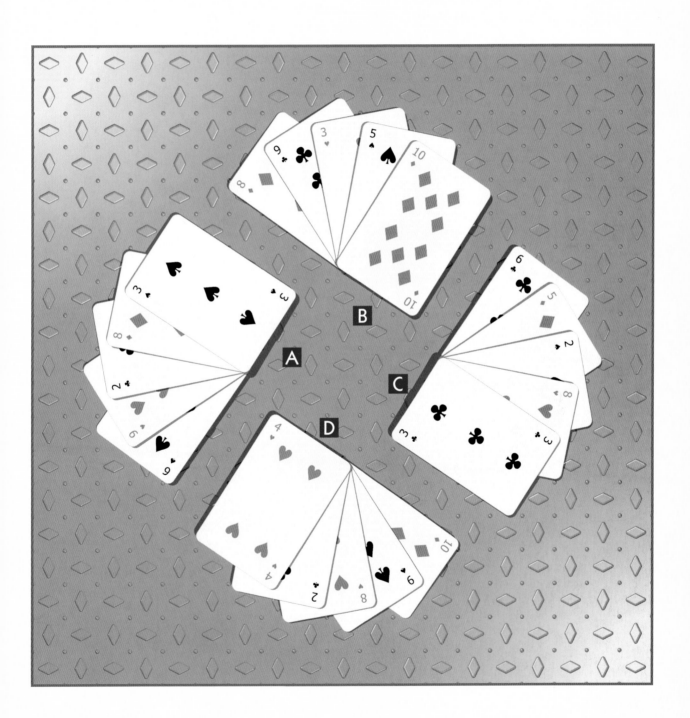

79 Place the seven cards on the numbered hexagons so the color of each curve matches.

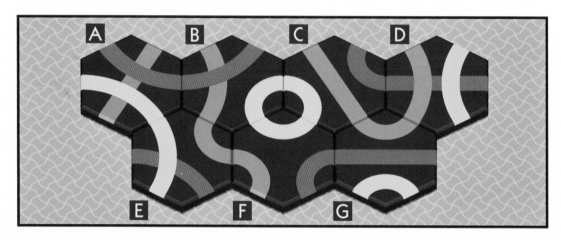

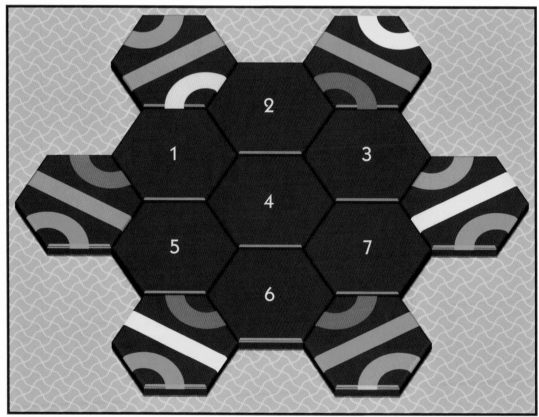

80 If you enter the tube at the arrow, where do you exit? The reverse side of the three different pieces is given in the small boxes.

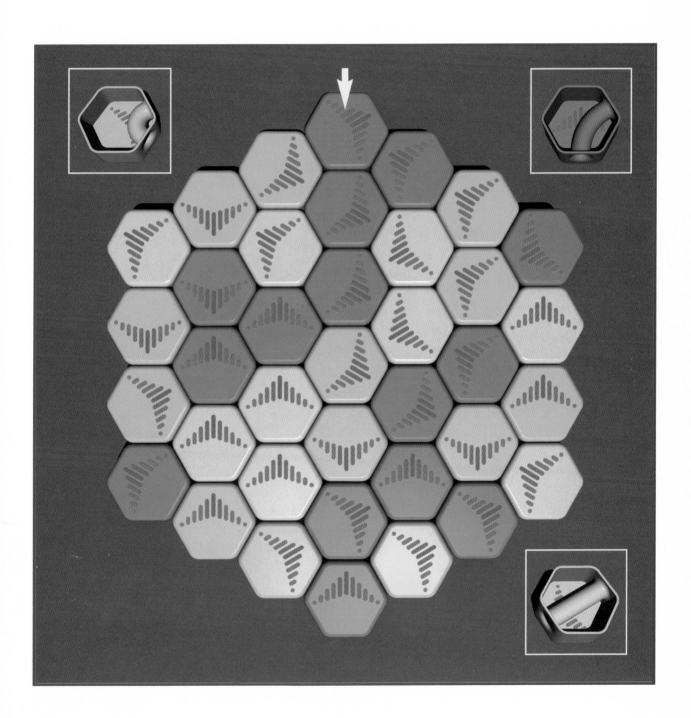

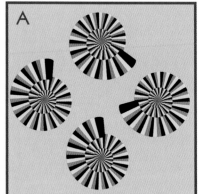

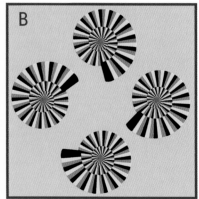

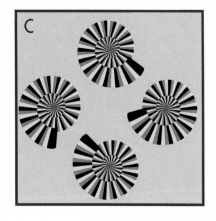

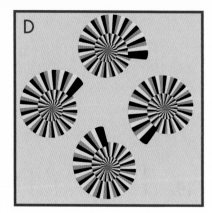

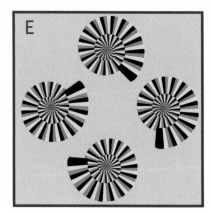

Which handles should be turned so that every column has only one disk with its yellow side up?

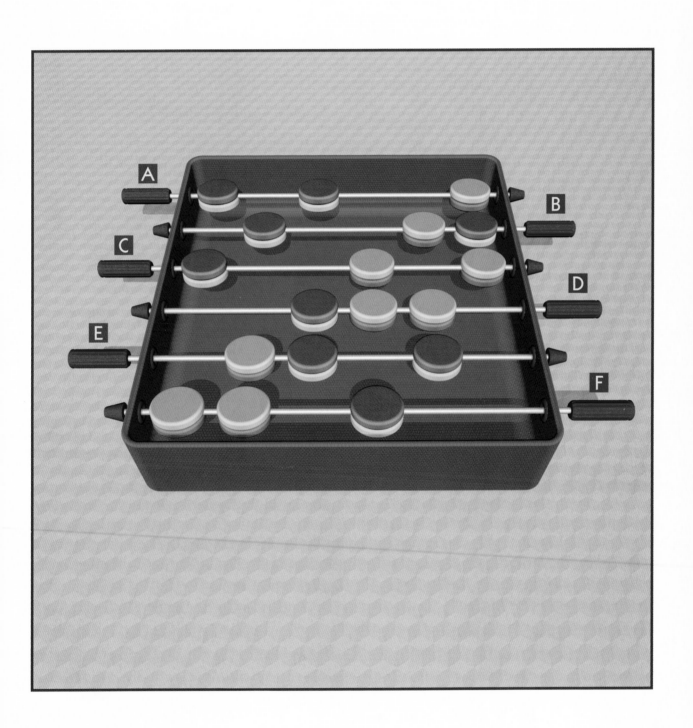

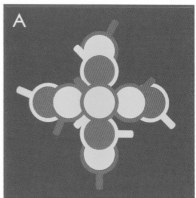

A

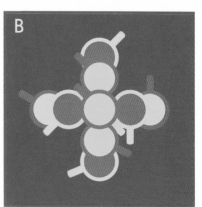

B

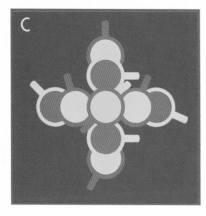

C

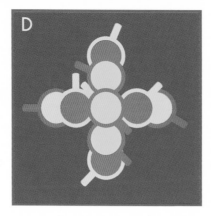

D

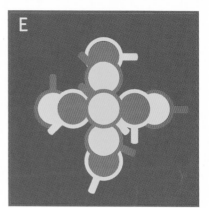

E

84 How many separate strands were woven into one?

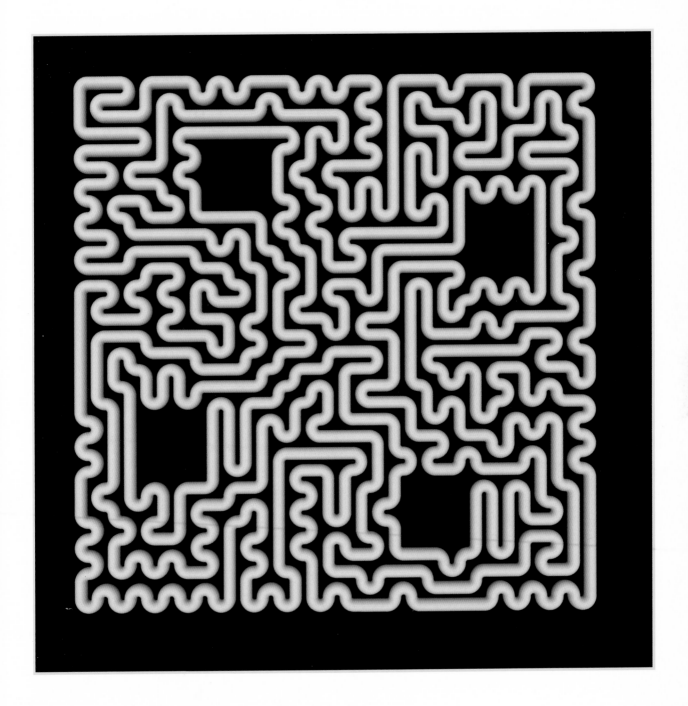

85 Each of the shapes in this picture can be paired up with another one the same shape but a different color. Pair them up!

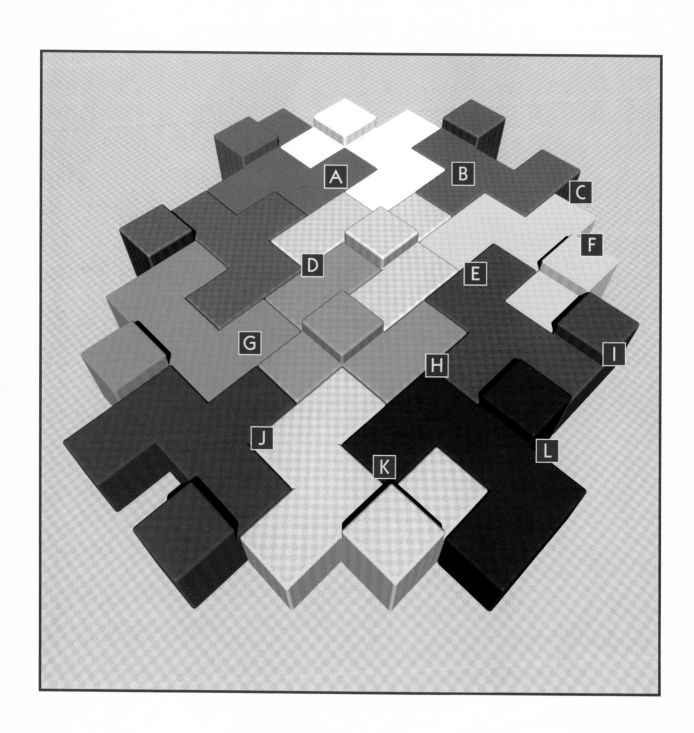

86 Portions of the letters of the words "THE END" are shown greatly enlarged. Pair up the lettered and numbered views.

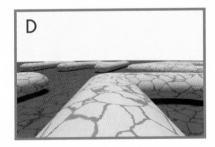

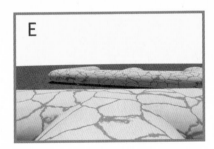

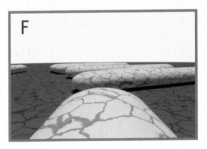

ANSWERS

1.

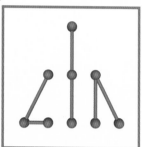

2. O.

3. Four.

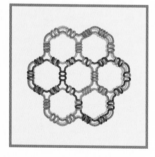

4. C-D-F.

5. From the bottom upward: B-C-A-D.

6. B-C-F-D-E-G-A-H.

7.

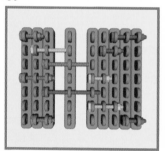

8.

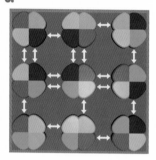

9. A-1, B-8, C-7, D-3, E-5, F-2, G-4, H-6.

10. A-C, B-E, D-F.

11.

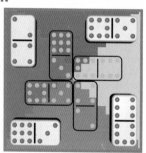

12. A-6, D-2.

13. Red.

14. A-E, B-H, C-G, D-F.

15. A-3, B-1, C-2.

16.

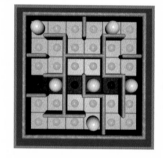

17. A-4, B-1, C-6, D-8, E-3, F-7, G-2, H-5.

18. They will turn in the same direction.

ANSWERS

19. 1-HAT, 2-ACE, 3-HIT, 4-LOT, 5-CAT, 6-COP, 7-SET, 8-PUT.

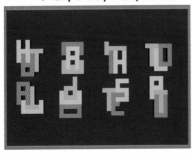

20. A-K, B-L, C-E, D-G, F-J, H-I.

21. A.

22.

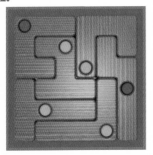

23. A-5, B-6, C-3, D-1, E-4, F-2.

24.

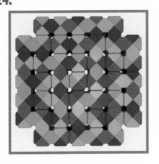

25. A-F, B-D, C-E.

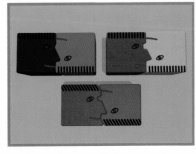

26. A-2, B-4, C-5, D-3, E-1.

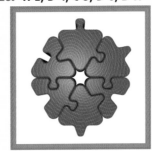

27. A-6, B-1, C-5, D-2, E-3, F-4.

28.

29.

30. Clockwise: middle-A-B-C-D.

31. A-3, B-1, C-2, D-4.

32. Two.

33.

34. A-4, B-2, C-3, D-1.

35. A-4, B-1, C-2, D-3.

93

ANSWERS

36.

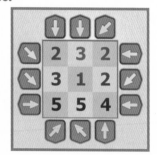

37.

38.

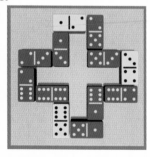

39. A-3, B-4, C-1, D-2.

40. A-3, B-7, C-2, D-6, E-1, F-5, G-4.

41.

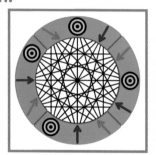

42.

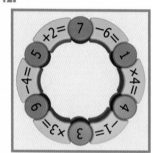

43. From the bottom upward: B-D-C-A-E.

44. Two remain: B and F.

45. From the bottom upward: B-I, A-D, C-L, E-K, F-H, G-J.

46. A-F-K, B-D-J, G-I-L, C-E-H.

47.

48. The order of the cuts: C-A-D-B.

49. A-2, B-6, C-3, D-1, E-5, F-4.

50.

51.

52. This requires a five-fourteenths turn counterclockwise.

53. A-3, B-5, C-6, D-1, E-8, F-2, G-4, H-7.

54. A-C, B-H, D-F, E-G.

55.

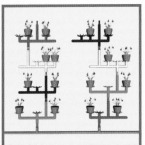

56. A-H-B-C-D-E-G-F.

57.

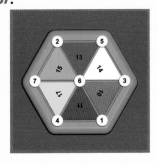

58. Opening the green taps causes twelve gallons of water to flow into each of the bottom two tubs.

59.

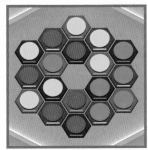

60.

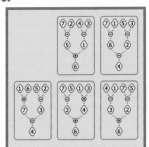

61.

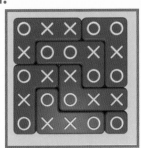

62. A-4, B-3, C-2, D-1.

63. Red = 1 lb., blue = 2 lb., yellow = 3 lb., green = 4 lb.

64.

65. A-4, B-2, C-3, D-1.

66. B.

67. D-C-A-B.
A: 180° + 270° + 270° = 720°,
B: 270° + 270° + 270° = 810°,
C: 90° + 180° + 270° = 540°,
D: 180° + 90° + 180° = 540°.

68.

ANSWERS

69.

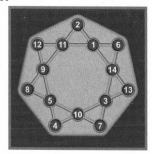

70. B.

71. A-1, B-4, C-3, D-2.

72. Three balls to the left goal (F, K, L); one ball to the right goal (I).

73. After 24 passes, the robot marked H will throw the ball into the basket.

74. A-F-H, B-D-I, C-E-G.

75. F-G-B-D-E-C-A.

76.

77.

78. Move the 6 of Spades from A to D, the 8 of Diamonds from B to A, the 3 of Clubs from C to B, and the 9 of Spades from D to C.

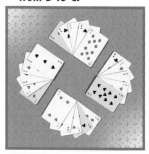

79. A-3, B-7, C-4, D-1, E-6, F-5, G-2.

80.

81. D.

82. C, D, F.

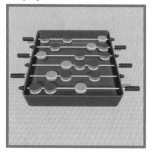

83. D.

84. Three.

85. A-F, B-K, C-J, D-I, E-H, G-L.

86. 1-C, 2-E, 3-A, 4-F, 5-B, 6-D.